Nation states are not as independent as is usually supposed. Their freedom of action is curbed by their inextricable involvement in a states system, and by the rules and institutions which they put in place to manage their relations. Watson's analysis is especially concerned with how the hegemonial authority of the richest and strongest powers also increasingly determines both the external and internal behaviour of nominally independent states.

After setting out the general framework of restraint imposed on states, the book looks in detail at attempts to limit national sovereignties in Europe by creating an overarching supranational authority, from Napoleon to the European Union. Outside Europe ex-colonial states have found their nominal independence limited by their inability to provide strategic security or economic well-being for their peoples. The aid they need subjects them to hegemonial pressures on economics, human rights and the environment.

Watson's analysis draws on his wide personal experience as a diplomat, historian and human rights worker. This book continues his landmark achievement of pushing the study of international systems beyond sovereign states to the realities of hegemony and supranational authority. Its highly readable style will appeal to scholars and the general public alike. A lively glossary will be of specific use to students.

Adam Watson is a former British Ambassador and Assistant Under-Secretary. He was also Director General of the International Association for Cultural Freedom and since 1978 he has been Professor of International Relations at the University of Virginia. He is the author of *The Evolution of International Society*.

D11145748

The Limits of Independence

Relations between states in the modern world

Adam Watson

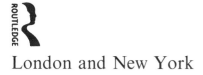

London and New York

First published 1997
by Routledge
11 New Fetter Lane, London EC4P 4EE

Simultaneously published in the USA and Canada
by Routledge
29 West 35th Street, New York, NY 10001

Typeset in Times by
BC Typesetting, Bristol
Printed and bound in Great Britain by
TJ International

British Library Cataloguing in Publication Data
A catalogue record for this book is available from the British Library

Library of Congress Cataloguing in Publication Data
A catalogue record for this book has been requested

ISBN 0–415–15811–7
      0–415–16907–0 (pbk)

To Douglas, Polly and Alaric

Contents

Acknowledgements

I owe a debt of gratitude to many people whose ideas and suggestions have helped me to write this book. This is particularly true for those on the brief list below, most of whom are quoted in the text.

George Kennan has given me constant encouragement, both by precept and by example, and has helped me to think more clearly about many of the book's themes. Barry Buzan expounded the concept of anarchophilia, and with characteristic perceptiveness has suggested a number of valuable improvements and corrections. Marion Dönhoff's writings exemplify the traditional Prussian virtues of personal integrity and religious and racial impartiality in government, which are echoed in this book. A.P. Rana provides an illuminating example of the Indian gift for coherent overview of the complexities of the international scene. Robert Jackson's work and conversation on quasi-states has enlightened the whole subject of small states and aid for me. Robert Wade-Gery was the first to explain the limitations of sovereignty to the British Committee for the Theory of International Politics, and in detail to me. Ole Waever showed me how my ideas on hegemony apply to contemporary Europe. Inis Claude clarified my understanding of how different from one another states are. I also wish to thank my publisher, Claire L'Enfant, for helping me to put this book into shape, and Heather McCallum for sympathetic and professional editing. Above all I want to thank my wife for her patient insistence on clarity and coherence.

Personal perspective

It is said that when someone reaches the age of eighty he or she is entitled, and perhaps is under a certain obligation, to look back at his or her experience and see what lessons can be drawn from it. In many societies this was the function of older people who had managed to survive and to retain their clarity of mind. In public life the concept of a senate (from the Latin *senex*, an old man) or council of elders derives from the awareness that the often bitter lessons of experience are one essential ingredient in the mix that makes for good judgement. But the past is not by itself a reliable guide to the future. It is not necessary that the advice of the elders should be followed: only desirable that it should be heard.

Of course in this age of specialization the only lessons worth offering to the public are those drawn from experience in one's field of competence. The views of eminent scientists about politics are worth no more than the views of eminent politicians about science. Some celebrities – famous actresses for example – can expect their general pontifications to command wide interest; but others do well to limit their offerings to the conclusions they have distilled from their own necessarily narrow area of expertise.

Most of my working life has been concerned with the practice and the theory of relations between states. Anyone born, as I was, at the beginning of the First World War can hardly feel that what are called international affairs have been conducted with great success. There was, and is, what scholars of the British school call an international society of states that conceive themselves as essentially independent; and that society has elaborate rules and institutions designed to manage order and change and lubricate relations between the states. The job was done adequately in the nineteenth century; and fairly adequately too in the half century since the Second World War came to an end. But the period from 1900 to 1945 was catastrophic. Events and public opinion in Europe span altogether out of the control of moderate statesmen. The wholesale decolonization of the last fifty years has had much less dislocating results and has brought considerable benefits; but we cannot feel complacent about it either.

Looking back on those events, and especially those with which I have been professionally involved, I have found myself increasingly pushed to the conclusion that international affairs have been, so to speak, too inter and too national. Have we cherished and idealized independence and sovereign statehood not wisely but too well?

That question is part of a wider set of doubts about the role of the sovereign state. Have Leviathan states (to use Hobbes's term) hogged too much power, too much administrative control, at the expense of both supranational and provincial political entities? Have sovereigns been too unwilling to countenance the devolution of their internal authority, and to accept what is now called the principle of subsidiarity? Externally, have they too often rejected supranational authority, which (as I will explain) I think must by its nature be hegemonial in practice?

Until fairly recently I supposed that we were living in an international society of essentially independent states. The world was shrinking, as the phrase went, and states were becoming more interdependent. But that did not really alter the nature of the states system. I assumed that the system, and the rules and institutions which the member states of international society had devised to manage the system, were in practice what they were understood to be in the Foreign Office, and in theory what Hedley Bull described them to be in his *Anarchical Society*.

My doubts about that picture began by my thinking about hegemony. The traditional British view of European history presumed that hegemony was undesirable. What mattered was to preserve independence and freedom for individual states. That could be done in two ways. Either you maintained a balance of power (the only alternative is an imbalance of power, said Nixon), which was realistic, but might not always be possible. Or you could aim to have a universal league, like the United Nations but strong enough and committed enough to multiple independences to stop an 'aggressor', which was idealistic and probably unattainable. But what if you doubt or question the basic assumption that independence is a good thing and hegemony a bad one?

The role of hegemony in systems of states took shape in my mind during the forty-year cold war. That struggle was a bipolar system dominated by two confrontational superpowers; and in its area each superpower exercised at least a hegemony. Martin Wight liked to describe the European society of states from its beginnings in the renaissance as a succession of hegemonies. I came to think that the enormous disparity of power between some states and others ensured that the strongest powers in *any* system of substantially independent states would in fact exercise some degree of hegemonial authority. Once I concluded that hegemony was an integral and inevitable feature of all such systems, then the concept of a system of independent states with no trace of hegemony at all seemed like infinity, a theoretical postulate which did not exist in practice.

Of course the degree of hegemony fluctuated. In the seventies and eighties, for instance, the authority of the United States in the non-communist world was diminishing, and the world was becoming 'more multipolar'. One could plot a graph of our non-communist world over a period of time according to the degree of hegemony. I thought it might be better to have two graphs. One would record the real inducements which the disparity of power enabled strong states to exercise in practice. The other would record the degree of hegemonial authority recognized by the institutions of the society – the nominal rights and responsibilities of various great powers such as permanent membership and a veto in the Security Council and now membership of the Group of Seven. I thought those graphs might be very useful to plot in detail. Some professional diplomats already had the broad thought in their minds.

One can draw a similar graph of hegemony right back through European history, with Napoleon as the peak. The Napoleonic experience shows that as the hegemony increases and the independence of the member states of the system diminishes, one passes over the line separating hegemony from dominion, and moves on beyond that towards a single imperial or universal authority. And it soon becomes clear that there is no real dividing line, but a spectrum ranging between two theoretical absolutes. All known historical patterns of managing the relations between a group of different political entities have shifted along this spectrum over time.

That period was also the age of wholesale decolonization. The anti-hegemonial view of European history went very well together with the post-imperial sentiment in Britain in favour of dissolving empires into independent states. The dislike of imperial authority can be considered as the extension to the rest of the world of the British anti-hegemonial policy towards Europe discussed in Chapter 3. But the devil is in the detail. When I became involved with the details of decolonization in the late 1950s and the 1960s, I began to doubt the wisdom, and even the practicability, of a policy based on the simplistic assumption that independent sovereign statehood was the only acceptable status for every territory in the world. Was there no intermediate status for those territories which had reached a stage of development and governmental experience where they could manage a substantial amount of local autonomy, but would not be able to stand on their own feet administratively or economically? St Helena was the example that used to come to my mind; but the question applies to much larger political entities as well. If such colonial states were unwilling to be wards of the former imperial power, or if the imperial power was unwilling to assume the task, could they be made general wards?

I had been encouraged, like many others concerned with decolonization, by the success of the Indian sub-continent since our withdrawal, and Indonesia since the departure of the Dutch. Of course colonialism brought economic advantages to the imperial power: that was its primary purpose. But the economic advantages need not be lost. Almost all the newly independent Asian countries (Indochina was the great exception) were showing that they could manage their own affairs: they were stable enough to enable our trade with them to continue. Asian decolonization did not seem to make us any worse off than we already were as a result of the war. Colonial administration seemed to me to have become not only much more costly than it had been, in money and blood and international ill-will, but also no longer necessary. After the French failure in Indochina, I thought it very statesmanlike of de Gaulle to withdraw from Algeria.

When I was head of the African side of the Foreign Office I was convinced that decolonization was the right course to follow, both for us and for the colonies. Some of my colleagues and others whom I respected thought otherwise. If we gave up our colonies and our strategic position in the Middle East, some of my British friends said, we would be driven back to our islands where we would starve, or at least suffer a calamitous fall in our standard of living. The same anxieties could be heard in France and Portugal. I did not share this fear. It seemed to me too close to the Marxist–Leninist theory of imperialism, that product of the nineteenth century idea that capitalist economies needed empires to thrive. After all, Japan and Western Germany weren't starving: they were moving forward from a much worse situation than ours to economic miracles. My conviction that colonial empire was no longer a paying proposition was reinforced when I was a secretary of the Africa Committee of the Cabinet, and heard the Prime Minister, Harold Macmillan, cogently express the same sceptical views. And in my meetings with French, Belgian and Portuguese officials concerned with Africa, I was glad to find several of them asking themselves the same questions.

From 1959 to 1962 I was fortunate to be given a unique assignment as a roving minister covering the area from Mauritania to the Congo, becoming ambassador to various French states as they became independent, and visiting British and Portuguese territories for comparison. I now think, in the light of hindsight, that I was too optimistic about the ability of the Western-educated African elites to run a modern state. Though the former dependent states of Asia have on the whole been a success since independence, in Africa they have been a disappointment to Westerners. At the same time I was impressed by the steadying effect of the administrative, technical, educational and other aid which the former imperial powers, especially the French, and other developed countries were willing to give to the new African states.

The French, much more than us, retained a presence and an authority in their former African colonies. Was this a form of hegemony, or an imperial relationship? The same question was in my mind during my years as ambassador to Cuba, a country which Fidel Castro was trying to move out of the American imperium in the Caribbean. But José Marti, who helped take Cuba from its previous status as a Spanish colony into the US imperium in the first place, used to quote the slave proverb 'To change masters is not to be free'. Fidel exchanged the US for the Soviet imperium. If Caribbean islands cannot stand on their own feet, I wondered what role other states do, and should, play in supporting them and telling them how they should be governed.

Thinking about hegemonial authority and post-colonial arrangements, I was increasingly aware of the key role which efforts to promote human rights now play in the general pattern of relations between states, especially between donors and recipients of aid. Did not these efforts amount to deliberate and systematic interference in the internal affairs of states and severely limit the newly acquired independence that their governments so prized?

My attention was directly focussed on this area when after leaving government service I became director–general of the International Association for Cultural Freedom, chairman of a co-ordinating committee for organizations concerned with refugees to Britain from Latin America, and an active member of the Swiss Fondation pour une Entraide Intellectuelle Européenne. How did the promotion of human rights, along with higher standards of living, education,

health and other such Western objectives, affect the many and conflicting responsibilities of governments? It became obvious to me that
human rights, which were earlier a part of what were called standards
of civilization, are an essentially Western concept, and have depended
more than anything else on the inducements and pressures applied by
the Western great powers. The governments of those powers in turn
are animated by non-governmental bodies and public opinion in
their countries. How in fact are economic and other standards of
well-being promoted across state borders by hegemonial authority?
And how does that hegemonial activity restrain and limit the sovereignty of weaker and poorer states?

In this book I have tried to offer an objective picture of the various
curbs on independence and sovereignty that now operate and have
operated in the recent past (remembering that past events and beliefs
operated in a different context) both in Europe and in the many
poorer and weaker states of the world. The book is intended as a contribution to the discussion of this ongoing and important issue. The
impersonal constraints resulting from inextricable involvement in a
system, and the rules put in place by member states to manage their
relations, are familiar enough. I have therefore concentrated my exam-
ination on hegemony and the recipient–donor relationship, in the hope
that this distillation of my experience will help to further our understanding of the limits of independence and the need for these limits,
in theory and in practice.

Adam Watson

1 The general framework

ATTITUDES TO INDEPENDENCE

This book is intended to discuss independence, and limits to it, as a way of organizing our present worldwide society of states. I want to look at specific restraints on the freedom of action of sovereign states, and the adequacy of those restraints, in the light of my experience in the twentieth century. I want to look at the relation of independence and hegemony to peace and order, and also to such standards of civilization as the environment and human rights. The book is not a disquisition on independence in the abstract or philosophically.

The present chapter provides a general framework within which we can examine specific aspects of the limits of independence. Those who have had the patience to read my *Evolution of International Society*,[1] and others who follow the academic literature on the subject, will be familiar with the concepts of a states system and an international society, and with terms like hegemony. I therefore do not need to define them again. For readers who are not so familiar with these concepts, I hope the brief summaries in the glossary will clarify the terms used in the book.

Here I will simply note that when a number of political entities are closely involved with one another, we call the group a **system of states** (as we speak of a solar system). The differing patterns of relationship between the states in a system range along a **spectrum** between two theoretical extremes: absolute independence of all the political entities involved, and the equally theoretical extreme of absolute, unitary centralization. All known systems, that is all the patterns of which we have any record, including the present global system and the European one from which it is substantially derived, lie somewhere along the spectrum. They contain elements both of independence, which gradually becomes more limited and diluted into local autonomy as one moves along the spectrum towards centralization or empire, and of imperial control which similarly becomes diluted into hegemonial authority when we move the other way.[2]

All international societies, including ours, impose certain **restraints** on the independence of their member states. In our global society the restraints are broadly speaking of three kinds. First there are those imposed by the fact of being locked into a **system** where each state is obliged to take account of the others and of the system itself – today particularly the economic pressures of the present system. In such a system unwise behaviour may carry very serious penalties. These impersonal restraints grow stronger as the net that holds the states together binds us all in an ever-increasing interdependence. Second there are the formal rules and institutions – the United Nations, international law, economic agreements, the diplomatic dialogue and so on – and the unwritten codes of conduct which the members of an **international society** of states consciously put in place to manage the pressures of the system. The machinery and prescribed behaviour define the legitimacy of an international society. But they do not necessarily make it orderly or safe by enforcing the rules. And third there are the limits imposed by the **hegemonial authority** of the strongest power or powers. In societies where the legitimacy is far towards multiple independences, hegemony is controversial; but it is always present. Today hegemony plays a major part in managing the affairs of our international society. We will examine the role of hegemony in more detail in the course of the book.

In the modern world of technology and interinvolvement it is becoming increasingly clear how necessary these restraints on independence are. Nevertheless all too many statesmen, the media and popular opinion glorify independence. Scholars of international relations see it as the constituent legitimacy of our time, which it still is. Many of them go on to declare, with much less justification, that it is an essential feature of an acceptable international society. The notion that independence is sacrosanct and the only acceptable status for members of an international society contradicts the historical evidence. The claim sometimes results from ignorance of history, which is all too common among scholars. Other academics and many politicians adopt a moral stance. Different arrangements, they say, may have existed in the past, and may then have been acceptable, but now and henceforth Independence with a capital 'I' is the right of every group that wants it. Any surrender of independence must be 'voluntary'.

Professor Barry Buzan pertinently defines the academic commitment to independence as follows:

> The third reason why basic questions about the core concept in the discipline remain not only unaddressed but almost unasked is anarchophilia, which is very much a consequence of ahistoricism and Eurocentrism. By anarchophilia, I mean the disposition to assume that the structure of the international system has always been anarchic, that this is natural, and (more selectively) that this is a good thing.[3]

Anarchy in this technical and theoretical sense does not mean disorder as such. It means a situation where political units refuse to acknowledge any higher authority. But one can lead to the other. The central problem posed by multiple independences, or as the theorists say, by the anarchical end of the spectrum, is an external one, how to maintain **international order**.

In the relations between states, and particularly where limitations of independence are concerned, there is an important theoretical and moral distinction between **coercion** and **voluntary agreement**. But in practice both are usually present in varying degrees. Between the naked force of military occupation practiced by Hitler and Stalin (even so, both used the thin disguise of puppet Quisling governments) and wholly free choice, a wide range of inducements and constraints help to shape a state's decisions about any partial surrender of its sovereignty. States may respond to the impersonal pressures, especially the economic constraints, of the tightening net that holds the world together. Other states or international institutions may offer or withhold compensating advantages. Is compliance with terms for the granting of aid, sometimes direly needed, always partly coercive and partly voluntary? Is that also true of a surrender of multiple independences to a wider centralizing authority, such as is now gradually happening in Europe? Does the distinction between coercive and voluntary refer to the decisions of governments, sometimes controlled by a small ruling elite, or to the opinions of the majority? This issue will crop up at various points in the book.

The values and assumptions that we now associate with multiple independences developed in Europe from the seventeenth century, and reached their peak in Europe and the Americas in the nineteenth. At the beginning of the twentieth century these values and assumptions were still paramount. But in the course of the century they have come under increasing challenge. In Europe we are witnessing a strong upsurge, or revival, of confederal tendencies towards major voluntary limitations of the independence of its member states. We will examine in the next chapter how this reaction in favour of supranational authority came about, and how the European Union has begun to operate as a collective hegemonial authority for the whole continent. Similarly the empires of the Europeans, including Russia, and of the Ottoman Turks have broken up into a number of independent or nominally independent fragments, all committed to sovereignty and as much freedom of action as possible. Yet after the first flush of nominal independence, a majority are becoming more aware how much they depend on outside support – economic, strategic and otherwise – and are working out ways of managing this dependence. Chapters 3, 4 and 5 are concerned with various limits to the freedom of action of formerly dependent states, and with the hegemonial authority of the major powers.

The nature of the relations between political entities in the world also continues to be transformed by the accelerating **technological revolution**. Technological innovation is an aspect of the economic dynamic that has propelled man to master the planet. Inventing tools and ways of doing things has been a characteristic of humankind since its beginnings. The process that has involved the whole world in a single economic and strategic system began in earnest with the development in Europe of printing, the cannon, the compass and the clock. This gave Europeans a certain economic and naval superiority outside Europe, though it still took Napoleon about as long as Hannibal to invade Italy across the Alps. The nineteenth-century industrial revolution and the twentieth-century technological one have provided us with instant communication, weapons with a worldwide range, and a rapid movement of goods and services that consumers everywhere can now obtain from everywhere else. The industrial and technological revolutions, and the consequent establishment of a global market, have been very largely driven by private enterprise exploring new and profitable potential. The subject is discussed further in Chapter 7. Until recently the immense technical transformation of human capacities radiated from Europe. But that is no longer the case; and Europe has shrunk back from its position of dominance to being an important but not the most dynamic area of the developed world.

LIMITS TO INDEPENDENCE IN EUROPE

We need to begin our enquiry in Europe for two reasons. First, our present international society was developed in Europe and spread by Europeans over the rest of the world, and it is still largely dominated by concepts of European origin. Second, the sense that the independent nation–state has been overtaken by history, and that states must now turn over a substantial degree of sovereignty to a supranational authority, has gone much further in Europe than anywhere else.

The highly original society of medieval Europe, before there were separate states in our sense, had a universal and very hierarchic structure. The renaissance shifted the practice of the society towards multiple independences, which became the accepted legitimacy of the new European international society established by the Westphalia settlement of 1648. The Westphalia settlement postulated an essentially non-hegemonial order for Europe, though it still retained considerable elements of unity and hierarchy. But there was a propensity to hegemony in the practice of the new nominally anti-hegemonial society of states. Order soon came to be maintained in Europe by the hegemonial authority of Louis XIV of France, the most powerful state in the system. It was a mild but single hegemony, exercised by a judicious mixture of diplomacy, money and the use of force, and operating wherever practicable within the framework of Westphalia. We will come again to the techniques and advantages of operating within an established legitimacy when we look at the mild but collective hegemony of the great powers today.

Could international order in Europe be non-hegemonial, as the Westphalia settlement postulated, as the legitimacy implied, and the precedent of the classical Greek city states apparently endorsed? At first the answer seemed to be no. Louis XIV soon established the hegemony of France. But after the anti-hegemonial coalition evoked by Louis' hegemony brought him down, for the best part of the eighteenth century the European society of sovereign princes related by blood or marriage was able to maintain a substantially non-hegemonial order, based on the Utrecht settlement of a **just balance of power**. The balance of power was designed to curb the freedom of action of the strongest, and to protect the weak princes against the strong ones. It was a way of managing an international society that was far towards the multiple-independences end of the spectrum. Because it was a collective and voluntary restraint, it was not always reliable; and it did not obviate the resort to force. Within the balance a degree of hegemony was exercised by two shifting and counterbalancing alliances. The abeyance of effective hegemonial authority was due in part to the temporary failure of France to realize its potential power relative to the other leading states. The revolution released springs of vitality in France, which under Napoleon was able to establish a dominion over much of Europe and hegemony in the European society as a whole.

Voltaire and Gibbon in the eighteenth century described Europe as '*une grande république*' divided into many states. Europe, in other words, was a **political and cultural unity**. It was in the matrix of European culture that the European states – mainly princes related by blood or marriage, their ministers and the few European republics – developed their international society.[4] During the formative centuries of the European society the great Muslim Ottoman empire ruled about a quarter of Europe and was a major economic, strategic and political player in the European states system; but it considered itself too alien to join the European society of princes, and was so considered by the Europeans. Separate rules and institutions were worked out to regulate its relations with Europe.[5] The distinction between the closely knit European society and the wider system raises the question how far our present worldwide society of states, and hegemonial authority in it, can transcend cultural differences.

After the defeat of Napoleon, order was maintained in the *grande république*, still a society of sovereign princes, by the collective hegemonial authority of the Concert of Europe: a concert of *all* the great powers in the society, not just the victors.[6] Other states could affect the working of the society in proportion to their influence and power – their weight in the system, or at least in that part of the system which mattered most to them – and were able to affect the discussions and action of the great powers accordingly. The Concert of Europe meant that the great powers accepted limits to their own freedom of action and imposed limits on other states. It produced order by providing flexible machinery for settling disputes and making adjustments, even if some adjustments were effected by the limited use of force. The governments of the great powers, in exercising their collective hegemony, had a sense of *raison de système*. That is, they felt responsible for the functioning of the European society of states as a whole: not always, or absolutely, but strongly enough to make it a rule of the game. When Metternich declared that '*Toute l'Europe est ma patrie*' he meant what he said.

Alas, the authority of the Concert of Europe to impose adequate limits on the freedom of action of its sovereign states steadily weakened as the nineteenth century progressed. The reasons why are discussed in the next chapter. In the first half of the twentieth century the international system was unmanageable. Voluntary restraint was not enough to prevent the double catastrophe of two world wars. The disaster produced a reaction in Europe against unfettered independence. Many Europeans today consider that Europe should be made into a real *grande république* with the voluntary but irreversible surrender of a much greater degree of national sovereignty to European central authorities than ever before, leaving little more than local autonomy for the states into which the European republic is divided.

The idea that there are necessary limits to the **external** behaviour of independent states is not new today, of course, and it was not new in 1815. In the middle ages, before there were what we would call states, those in authority were restrained, in varying degrees, by what they accepted as the laws of God and the rules of chivalry. In the renaissance, that age of unbridled princely behaviour, the Medici and others saw the advantage to themselves and other Italian rulers that the affairs of Italy should remain in a certain balance, and that it would pay them to uphold that balance by money and arms. The idea of restraint was conspicuously present in Grotius' concept of a code of international law binding sovereigns in their dealings with each other. Restraints on independence underlay the Covenant of the League of Nations and the United Nations Charter. The loose commitments accepted by states in these universal documents, and the more binding ones in specific treaties between allies, nevertheless leave independent states with the capacity to disregard their commitments if they so decide. Most of the sovereign states of our international society have acted in accordance with their commitments most of the time. Butterfield and Wight formulated the concept as 'the principles of prudence and moral obligation which have held together the international society of states throughout its history, and still hold it together'.[7] But when the chips go down, action in accordance with the commitments is voluntary. What surprises many Europeans today, looking with rueful hindsight at the ruin of their continent, is that responsible statesmen in the early part of this century could think that European civilization had progressed to the point where voluntary restraint alone was adequate to prevent disaster.

The corresponding concept, that there should be limits to the **internal** freedom of action of a ruler or government towards its subjects, goes back to the earliest civilizations where rulers were regarded as agents of a deity, and did not have 'a right to govern wrong'. In Europe the idea that domestic misgovernment or tyranny can reach a point where other governments have an obligation to intervene also goes back to medieval practice. It has played a significant and growing role in the development of the European and especially the present worldwide society of states. The licence to govern as they liked assumed by renaissance princes, and the live and let live attitude of non-interference which became the rule during the centuries when the European society of states was a princes' club, held intervention tightly in check. But the French Revolution proclaimed the right and duty to interfere in the name of liberty, which Napoleon interpreted as a free hand to remodel and 'regenerate' the domestic government of territories under his imperial control. After Napoleon's defeat the Concert of Europe continued this policy in more moderate ways. It asserted and fulfilled, not a right to interfere but rather what it saw as the obligation to enforce acceptable government in other states by bringing pressure on them. When other inducements failed, the pressure culminated in armed intervention: which costs both money and blood.

However, the practice of the European society of states changed with the times. In nineteenth-century Europe powerful new forces were working against both external and internal limits to independence. The main thrust came from a triad of closely interlocked and mutually reinforcing aspirations: sovereignty, democracy and nationalism. It has been said that the worship of abstract nouns has been the cause of more misery in the world than the worship of all the graven images since the origin of humankind. These three nouns are still idolized. Together they can induce a dangerous public frenzy. In the nineteenth century they gained ground fitfully, and more in some states of the European society than others. But as the century progressed, they increasingly weakened the restraints and limits on the freedom of action of Europe's member states, and pushed the society away from being a single *grande république* towards the anarchical extreme of the spectrum. By the beginning of the twentieth century liberals, and indeed a majority of public opinion in Europe and North America, regarded the triad of aspirations as progressive, and bracketed most restraints on independence together with other features of early nineteenth-century government as Metternichian and reactionary. We will need to look at each aspiration when we examine the European scene in the next chapter.

In the twentieth century the picture became more complex. Statesmen in the more sophisticated states were dismayed by the recent failures of their international society, and particularly by the horrors of the First World War. They realized that the society of states, now worldwide, had been allowed to grow altogether too anarchical for its own survival. Led by President Wilson, the Western victor powers after the First World War opted to restore a modest degree of collective hegemony. It was to be exercised, not by all the great powers, but by those that the victors deemed responsible.[8] Also unlike the Concert of Europe the hegemonial powers would act in association with the other sovereign states in the world in a League of Nations. The provisions of the League Covenant were a step away from anarchical licence. Those who thought like Wilson hoped that these flimsy arrangements would make the world safe for democracy, and also for sovereignty and nationalism. But the mere existence of institutions and rules does not ensure their effectiveness. In fact the proposed concert of good powers did not materialize.

The tradition of the European *grande république* thus provided for the sovereignty of princes, with varying degrees of limitation in practice. In the first half of the twentieth century the limits of independence were too loose to prevent a twice-repeated catastrophe. Many Europeans since then have come to see their traditions in a different light, and are working to create a federal Europe which would supersede sovereign nation–states. We will examine the process in the next chapter.

EXPANSION AND WITHDRAWAL OUTSIDE EUROPE

The second aspect of worldwide interinvolvement that sets the frame for our discussions is the establishment in the rest of the world of states on the European model. Those states were almost all established as colonial dependencies, and the few Asian polities that were not formally colonized were remodelled on European lines. Now, with surprisingly little change, they make up the majority of the nominally independent states of our international society.

Since the time of Columbus Europeans have been engaged in competitive imperial expansion. The expansion was mainly but not entirely for economic reasons, and was conducted very largely by traders and settlers. Before that, Europeans had for millenia conducted a desultory trade with the high civilizations of Asia through Middle Eastern intermediaries; these Asian civilizations also traded and fought with each other. But such economic and strategic contacts were too sporadic and marginal for us to include Greco-Roman Europe and the high Asian civilizations in a single meaningful system of states.

When European traders and settlers expanded outside Europe in earnest, European states became involved in order to protect them. The technical superiority which made the European empires possible gradually integrated the dependent states of those empires and the remaining independent areas outside Europe for the first time into an interdependent economic and strategic whole, a single system of European-type states. Some non-European areas became specialized producers for a more developed market and omnivorous consumers of all the technically advanced goods and services that the developed market offered in return.

The European states, in order to manage their competitive involvement, also gradually brought the whole world to accept their international society of states. At first the system east of Europe had separate rules, largely formulated by Asians; but the Europeans eventually tried to manage it by extending the rules and institutions of the grande république, including independence. Not only the individual states, but the framework of our contemporary international society also, were unmistakably made in Europe.

The maritime states on the western fringes of Europe had much the same attitudes to international relations. The traditional English approach was akin to Venetian, Portuguese and Dutch practice. All four were maritime trading members of the European grande république. Their geographical position and their commercial commitment outside Europe led them to develop a dual policy. Inside the commonwealth of Europe all four wanted their traders and settlers to operate safely, and wanted the hands of the state free to protect them. The maritime states needed to ensure that they and their international society were not dominated by a hegemonial state; they therefore favoured a multiple mobile balance of power, consciously maintained, and adjusted as the relative power of the member states changed.[9] But outside Europe, across the salt sea, the Portuguese, Dutch and British trading communities established maritime empires. Their eastern imperial ventures were at first merely zones of trade and influence established by licensed private commercial companies in areas of very different cultures, like India, China and Japan. In some of those zones, particularly India and the southeastern islands, the companies gradually acquired increasing administrative commitments (later taken over by the states) in order to ensure the kind of order that would permit their commercial enterprises to flourish. Venice, Portugal, the Netherlands and England thus resembled commercial city–states of former times.[10] The Spanish and French empires were similar but always more imperial in intent, with private enterprise playing an active but more subordinated role.

A significant feature of the European imperial framework is that the power on the other margin of Europe, namely Romanov Russia during the two centuries from Peter the Great to the Revolution, was also anti-hegemonial towards the *zapad* or West and imperialist in the Ottoman empire and Asia. Rivalry in Asia and contrasting political systems made the governments in St Petersburg and London into imperial opponents most of the time, but great crises like the struggles against Napoleon and the German Reich brought them into uneasy alliance to prevent a hegemony in Europe. As the United States inherited much of Britain's world role, it found itself in an analogous relation to the Soviet Union. The two powers were in brief reluctant alliance against Hitler, but in superpower opposition at other times and elsewhere.

The competitive empires[11] of the maritime powers, together with those of Spain, France and Russia, between them integrated the rest of the world into the pressures and interests of the European states system. In so doing, they severely limited the sovereignty of the dependent states in their empires. But on the other hand the policies of the maritime powers and Russia kept Europe itself far towards the multiple independences end of the spectrum. The powers that favoured a greater political integration of Europe were, not surprisingly, those at the centre.

DISSOLUTION OF THE EUROPEAN EMPIRES

The great tide of decolonization, which brought political independence to the states established by the Europeans outside Europe, has more radically changed the nature of our global states system than any other development of the twentieth century. The immense areas concerned were inhabited by peoples with very different cultural traditions. The Ottoman Empire for long excluded itself from the society of European states, although it was half in Europe and also an heir to Mediterranean civilization. Many Asian civilizations were much more different, both from Europe and from each other. But because the colonial states which achieved independence were modelled on those of Europe, and had governments formed by Western-educated elites, it seemed reasonable to apply without much modification the rules and assumptions which our international society inherited from the Europeans.

When the century of unprecedented peace and prosperity in Europe was shattered by the catastrophe of World War I, the ebb tide of European imperialism set in. Thoughtful Europeans became uncomfortably aware that their culture, and certainly their dominance, was finite, like other cultures before them. Kipling wrote, 'Lo, all our pomp of yesterday\Is one with Nineveh and Tyre'. Spengler's seminal *Decline of the West* and Toynbee's *Study of History* held that cultures or civilizations rather than individual states were the determining units of world history, and diffused the idea that European culture and power were in decline. The new Wilsonian international society was somewhat more sensitive to the needs and rights of subject peoples and different cultures than the previous era of European dominance had been. But international practices and standards did not yet seem multicultural to Europeans, or to Western-educated elites. The League of Nations, international law, world commerce, all seemed firmly in Western hands.

The European empires effectively disintegrated into multiple independences only after the Second World War. The recent dissolution of the Russian empire virtually completed the process. Decolonization has not diminished global integration: on the contrary, technological advance, economic liberalization and great power hegemony are still drawing the net tighter. What decolonization did was to treble the number of sovereign states recognized by international society: almost all of them former European dependences. In international society today all member states are presumed to be wholly independent. The only available or at any rate the only acceptable status for the decolonized states, in law and theory, is full sovereignty and juridical equality with other member states. The fundamental legitimacy on which the elaborate structure of the society's rules and institutions rests is far towards the multiple independences end of the spectrum of possible arrangements, and deliberately far from the imperial end.

The meaning of terms like independence has to be stretched unreasonably to fit all the new cases. The enormous disparities in size, wealth and experience, in degree of social development, and in cultural traditions, make for a reality so different from the legitimacy that it has produced serious strains. Chapter 3 discusses the significance of this great fragmentation of our international society. Chapter 4 looks at some of the problems of ministries that are inadequate in size, resources and experience to fulfil the role postulated for them.

STANDARDS OF CIVILIZATION

The great powers who constituted the Concert of Europe were later joined by the United States and Japan. Their sense that they had a responsibility to ensure a minimum of what they sincerely believed to be good government developed into the later nineteenth-century concept of standards of civilization. The powers insisted on conformity to their standards, particularly in non-European countries, culminating in their collective armed intervention in China in 1900.

The Western powers' sense that it is their responsibility to induce, and where necessary and practicable to enforce, minimum standards remains vigorous. Current Western standards of civilized behaviour include our expanding concept of human rights and the protection of the environment. These collective limits to internal independence provide a substitute for the imperially imposed restraints which have now been swept away by decolonization. They have a considerable impact on the functioning of international society and on the domestic government of most of its member states. The issues will be discussed in Chapter 5.

As a result of the two world wars and the additional strains imposed on the international society by decolonization and increasing interdependence, we in the West are beginning to see the need for greater restraints more clearly, and to welcome them more than we recently did. The inadequate legal and universal machinery of restraint – the United Nations, international law and so on – remains in place. But we now rely less on it to limit the economic and strategic freedom of states to act in ways which other states consider irresponsible. The great powers, especially the United States, have effective carrots and sticks which they can and do use to induce other states to conform to what they consider acceptable behaviour. Chapters 5 and 6 discuss the authority and responsibilities of the larger hegemonial powers, especially of the United States, now the only power with an effective global reach. Chapter 5 looks at the hegemonial pressures brought to bear by the great powers to make the governments of smaller states observe minimum standards; Chapter 6 discusses responsibility and moral obligation more generally.

TWO SETS OF QUESTIONS

We are left with two sets of questions. The first concerns changes in the relations of essentially independent states in a more integrated but still international society. To what extent does this society now tend to rely on the hegemonial pressures which the great powers can bring to bear? How does that reliance affect the responsibilities – the prudent management and the moral obligation – of the major powers? Can an effective hegemonial concert be multicultural? How far is our practice shifting, as the large number of small and weak powers come to expect more from international society, and are learning the techniques of getting it? How far will our changed practice in due course pull our sense of legitimacy also along the spectrum away from multiple independences?

The second set of questions concerns our manner of looking at the structure of our society of states, and at the differing ways in which the great range of political entities function in it. Are our assumptions of sovereignty and multiple independences, our concept of 'international' relations, no longer adequate to describe today's realities, including the pressures of the kinetic and increasingly autonomous world economy? These questions are being asked more insistently by theorists of what are still called international relations. We do not have the answers. My suggestions are in Chapter 7.

NOTES

1 Adam Watson, *Evolution of International Society*, Routledge, 1992.
2 It is convenient to give the theoretical extreme of absolute military centralization its traditional name of a universal empire, though the term has pejorative overtones. Some scholars call the theoretical ends of the spectrum anarchy and hierarchy.
3 From Buzan and Little, *Introduction to International Relations*, Oxford University Press, forthcoming. The core concept in the discipline, mentioned in the quotation, is defined as the idea of an international system. I quite agree that anarchophilia is a consequence of ahistoricism and eurocentrism. Together they amount to using too short a time frame of reference, and too limited a cultural context, for an understanding of how systems of states work.
4 The sovereigns that made up the grande république were as quarrelsome as the city states of classical Hellas or the classical Indian kingdoms described in the Arthashastra, both of which also developed societies of substantially independent states within a common culture. But the European princes were less 'foreign' to each other, more a family, than the Greek cities or the Indian kings.
5 On the separate nature of Ottoman relations with Europe please see my *Evolution of International Society*, pp. 216–18.
6 The great powers that managed the Concert of Europe from 1815 were Britain, Russia, Austria, Prussia and France.
7 Herbert Butterfield and Martin Wight, eds, *Diplomatic Investigations*, Allen & Unwin, 1966, p. 13.
8 I am reminded of Mark Twain's remark that the world is divided into the good guys and the bad guys, and the good guys get to decide which is which.
9 England (after 1707 Great Britain) did not take part in the Westphalian settlement, but it opposed the successive bids for hegemony of the Habsburgs, Louis XIV, Napoleon and the German Reich, and played a major anti-hegemonial hand in the settlements of Utrecht, Vienna and Versailles. So too the Dutch house of Orange, like the Corinthians in classical Greece, regularly and dangerously supported the weaker side against the stronger to redress the balance.

10 A useful analysis of city–states and the forces which drive them is contained in Charles Tilly's *Coercion, Capital and European States AD 990–1990*, Blackwell, Oxford, 1990.

11 The educated gentlemen who played this great game knew that their complex dual system of relations between states was not the only one. They were keenly aware of the historical parallels. In particular they were steeped in the classics, which offered as precedents the anti-hegemonial policies of the city–states, the imperial experience of Rome, and the Hellenistic mixed pattern of kingdoms and autonomous cities which most resembled the European pattern. They regarded Europe much more as a unity than did the populist leaders of the first half of the twentieth century. They knew and agreed with Gibbon's dictum that 'a philosopher may be permitted to consider Europe as one great republic', but they wanted that republic to be as 'balanced' and non-hegemonial as possible. On the other hand they accepted that beyond the cultural divide different rules and practices were required, even with the high civilizations of Asia.

2 The European imbalance of power or the German question

Against the background of the generalities in the previous chapter we can now consider in more detail what restraints there were on the independence of the European states, and how much the steady erosion of those restraints contributed to the calamitous wars of the first half of this century. We can also look at alternative options for organizing the society of European states, and the growth of awareness that firmer limits to the freedom of action of states are necessary to avoid further disaster.

THE ANARCHIC EUROPEAN SOCIETY OF STATES

A great deal has been written about the origins and causes of the First World War, that devastating explosion which inflicted incalculable political, economic, cultural and genetic damage on European civilization, but scarcely harmed the rest of the world and indeed hastened its emancipation from European dominance. The literature on the subject ranges from the polemical to the studiously impartial; and over the whole range it is suffused by a sense of guilt and shame. Many writers have pointed out that several obstinate disputes between the leading European states in the years before the war were settled by diplomatic bargaining, and that the remaining issues could have been settled as well. These writers therefore go on to discuss the more fundamental causes of the conflict. Serious scholars as well as polemicists have declared that the root cause of the catastrophe, or at any rate the essential condition which made it possible, was what Sir Norman Angell called the international anarchy. That condition was the independence of powerful sovereign states with no restraint on their actions save their own sense of responsibility, coupled with a general opinion that in such an anarchic system war was the *ultima ratio* of governments – a rational and therefore permissible last resort.

To see international anarchy as the sole or the principal cause of a major explosion like the First World War is a gross oversimplification, like other single-cause explanations. Indeed the 'English school' of international relations – Manning, Butterfield, Wight and their successors, including myself – has been concerned to show that, although the international society of Europe had for centuries been anarchic in the technical sense of having no supranational authority, and had enshrined its multiple independences in the legitimacy of sovereignty, it was for most of the time in fact adequately managed.[1] Yet anarchy did provide the setting for the appalling damage which the Europeans then inflicted on each other. So we need to ask what other structure of the society might have helped to prevent or mitigate the two successive disasters. Moreover as we tackle today the imposition of effective and acceptable limits on the independence of European states, our experience over the last two centuries is one of our most useful guides. Much of that experience is a cautionary tale, warning us which curbs proved ineffective.

THE WEAKENING OF RESTRAINT

In the previous chapter we noted a triad of revolutionary popular aspirations which weakened restraint and authority in the European society of states: sovereignty, democracy and nationalism.

Of the three aspirations, **sovereignty** is the most directly related to independence. The word and the concept derive significantly from the rights of sovereign princes. In its ultimate form it implies the legitimation of a ruler or a state to act as it sees fit, both internally towards its subjects and externally towards other states. Internally it carries the corollary that sovereigns should not interfere in each others' domestic affairs. Externally states are committed to operate within a framework of international law and the treaty obligations they have freely entered into with other states. But untrammeled sovereignty means that there should be no supranational authority capable of enforcing either general rules or individual contracts. In fact there was no longer such an authority in Europe in the second half of the nineteenth century, and there is no very effective one in the world as a whole today. Sovereignty and independence, in other words, imply an anarchical society in the technical and in the colloquial sense. The belief that 'this is a good thing' is what Buzan aptly calls anarchophilia.

Democratization spread in Europe throughout the nineteenth century in much the same way as sovereignty: fitfully and at a very different pace in different countries. In that century it was largely an aspiration of the literate middle class to elect governments responsible to the will of the people, the general will. As the population of a state became its citizens, participating more in the political process, democracy gave them greater control over how their government acted. Internally, democratization limited the arbitrary power of governments to oppress the majority of their subjects; but it also sometimes increased the tyranny of the majority. Externally, democratization took the conduct of relations between states out of the hands of a cosmopolitan upper class. Aristocratic statesmen were often cynical and acquisitive; and many of them acquired by birth an authority which they were not competent to discharge. Internally the liberal polemic against aristocratic rule may have been largely justified. But internationally the abler aristocratic statesmen understood, and taught the others, *raison de système* and the value of restraint, and the need not to push too far their quarrels with their neighbours and partners. The spread of democracy removed one set of restraints on wilful behaviour without replacing it by another.

This is not to say that democracy is an undesirable form of government. On the contrary, it is one of the great threads of European and Western history, and a practice to which most Westerners, and certainly I myself, are deeply committed. Democracy, and the restraints and tolerances that its successful operation requires, are a political habit which is slow to grow and become generally accepted. But when as in the latter half of the nineteenth century, it is fused with sovereignty that admits no restraint outside itself and with national passion, it can produce an intoxicating and dangerous brew.

Nationalism is a protean word that takes many different shapes at various times and places. In the west of Europe nationalism developed within the boundaries of existing states, rather than round a language or ethnic group. Thus the *nation française* included some German, Italian and Basque speakers, but not all those who spoke French. But in the eastern half of the *grande république*, where the loyalties of the middle class to a particular state were less developed or nonexistent, nationalism was more strictly linguistic; and in the Ottoman Empire it was linguistic and religious. Nineteenth-century nationalists held that those who spoke or even formerly spoke a common language constituted a *Volk* or *popolo*. They demanded that each Volk should be incorporated in an independent state that included as far as possible all its members. This programme involved jettisoning the elaborate balance which the states of European society had carefully worked out for themselves, and drastically reconstituting those states to correspond to Volk and linguistic boundaries. Since these boundaries were fuzzy and overlapping where they could be said to exist at all, drastic transfers of population or sizeable 'national minorities' were bound to result. The conflicting aims of the nationalists were not a recipe for peace. Like the corresponding aims during the earlier wars of religion, they seemed to their proponents more important than peace.

The anarchic tendency of the European society towards multiple independences had been built into its basic legitimacy at Westphalia and reaffirmed at Utrecht and by eighteenth-century practice. The tendency was aggravated by nationalism and increasing public control of foreign relations. Most of the independent states into which the *grande république* was divided became increasingly responsive to popular passion and increasingly irresponsive to anything outside themselves and the interests of their state or group. Nationalism spread downward to the point where by the beginning of the twentieth century the great majority of Europeans west of Russia were animated by nationalist fervour of one kind or another, and in Russia the internationally conscious sections of the population equally so. The European international society became increasingly disintegrated: that is, the restraints which held the multiple independences in check became steadily less effective. *Raison d'état* gave way to what may be called *passion d'état*.

Not all Europeans were caught up in nationalist enthusiasm. Many who held to earlier or more aristocratic traditions, many scholars and many members of the Jewish communities considered linguistic nationalism to be absurd as well as pernicious. Bismarck said that an individual's nationality was the result of what he was taught at school. Spengler in a passage that is relevant to our enquiry wrote in 1922:

> The scientific presentation of history was distorted throughout the nineteenth century by a notion derived or at least developed by the Romantic movement, the idea of the *Volk* in the moral-enthusiastic sense. Whenever in earlier times a new religion or decorative art or architecture or script appears, or indeed a new empire or great destruction, researchers phrase their question: what was the Volk that produced this phenomenon? To ask a question . . . so false in every detail must evoke the wrong image of the events. 'The Volk' as the basic form in which people have achieved anything in history, the original home, the migrations of 'the' Volk, reflect the great upsurge of the idea of the [French] nation in 1789 and the [German] Volk in 1813. But because this idea is so full of

emotion, it escapes criticism. . . . For us today world history means the history of this and that Volk. Everything else – culture, art, language, religion – is supposed to be created by Völker. The state is a form of the Volk. I want to demolish this romantic notion. The earth has been inhabited since the ice age by human beings, not Völker. . . . The origin and development of the genetic and linguistic sides of a given population are quite unconnected.[2]

1800–1820: ALTERNATIVES FOR EUROPE

The epilectic convulsions which overtook Europe twice between 1914 and 1945 occured after a century which can be seen in retrospect as a long period of relative peace, prosperity and progress. The nineteenth-century European international society was able to manage a series of fairly orderly adjustments to changing pressures. Those adjustments involved some minor resorts to force in the mid century, but did not interfere with spectacular material advances, the spread of democracy and the expansion of European domination over the rest of the world.

A rigid determinist would say that the European society of states could not have developed otherwise than it actually did. But in periods of flux, especially after major wars, several options are usually possible; and the statesmen in a position to take decisions are almost oppressively conscious of the range of options. It is worth looking at other ways in which Europe might have developed, and keep them in mind when we look at the contemporary scene. While we do so we should hold in suspense the depressing conclusion that the two catastrophic wars were inherent in the very structure of the society, and inescapable because the nature of that structure could not be changed, and that nothing acceptable to the popular will of the peoples of Europe could have prevented them.

The settlement agreed at Vienna after the Napoleonic wars was not the only available one. Broadly speaking, three other ways of organizing the *grande république* were in the minds of statesmen as alternative outcomes of the flux of war at the beginning of the nineteenth century. We need to examine them with reference to the way the European society of states is being reorganized today. The three options particularly concerned the political and economic administration of central Europe, the area between France and Russia which was mainly inhabited by Germans and Italians. The options offered a choice of ways to deal with the problem that increasingly confronted Europe during the nineteenth century and which laid waste the continent in the first half of the twentieth: namely the German question.

Before the 1860s European statesmen thought in terms of three 'Germanies' within the Holy Roman Empire and its successor after 1815, the *Deutsche Bund*. These were: Austria and the house of Habsburg, always a major power; Prussia, also a major power but less so; and what the French called '*la troisième Allemagne*', the remaining smaller client states. Some of these client states were usually allied to France and others to the Habsburgs, the two imperial powers of Europe. Prussia and the troisième Allemagne merged in 1871 to form the second Reich; and from then on economic and military power in the centre of the continent grew disproportionately, especially in the new German Reich but also to a lesser extent in Austria–Hungary. The relatively faster development of central European strength was legitimate and praiseworthy in itself. But if left unchecked it would result in a hegemonial imbalance of power, that the two central powers were very ready to exploit but which would be unacceptable to the other great powers of Europe. How to manage the new imbalance of power has been the twentieth-century form of the German question.

The Napoleonic option

The first alternative way of organizing Europe was what we may call the Napoleonic option, with a range of minor modifications. It is interesting to us for two reasons. Napoleon actually put it into practice, which enables us to see its strengths and weaknesses. Also it has acquired a special significance because it is the organization of Europe which most resembles the present and projected European Union.

Napoleon did not promulgate his imperial design in advance, but expanded it piecemeal as opportunities offered and so far as his continual wars allowed. It conformed to the usual pattern. There was a directly administered bureaucratic empire proper at the centre, extending to a periphery of subordinate satellite states (Holland, Bavaria, Italy, Spain, etc.), and beyond that to independent states over whose external relations he came to exercise a hegemonial authority (Prussia, Austria, Denmark, etc.). The total area was gradually amassed and integrated until it came to include everything between the English Channel and Russia. 'Napoleon progressively centralized control of his empire until he seemed bent on founding a European government in which national states had no part.'[3] Napoleon's imperial design pushed the organization of the European society of states far along the spectrum away from multiple independences towards a centralized control which in his case was indeed an empire in the conventional sense.

Napoleon also transformed the internal social structure of Europe. He wrote to his brother that 'the peoples of Germany, of France, of Italy, of Spain, want equality and value liberal ideas'. Acting on this belief he changed the social structure of central Europe as the Revolution had changed that of France, opening up opportunities for the middle class. The more realistic central Europeans, especially among those engaged in manufacturing and trade, rallied in impressive numbers to the new dispensation. Because of the advantages that it offered to them, they accepted the political, cultural and most notably economic predominance of France that Napoleon insisted on. By 1811 some two thirds of the *grande armée* that he assembled to invade Russia was composed of non-Frenchmen, often under their own officers. In time the empire, had it survived, would have become a multiethnic and administratively multilingual structure, open to talent from all Europe, with a Bonaparte–Habsburg dynasty, Paris as its effective capital, French as its imperial language, and Rome as a ceremonial legitimation echoing the Holy Roman Empire of Europe's past.[4]

Napoleon's imperial design encountered two principal internal difficulties. First, it was imposed by force of arms. Second, although his autocracy was considered by many in the middle class to be enlightened, it opposed the triad of their aspirations, especially linguistic nationalism and a democratic say in government. How long would the advantages which his rule offered to individuals have kept the non-Frenchmen, whose support his régime needed, from espousing those aspirations? In fact what made Germans turn from him in large numbers after 1812 was not his failure to satisfy their aspirations but his military defeat. Looking back at the Napoleonic attempt to impose a single imperial design on continental Europe, we can discern premonitions both of Hitler's imperial tyranny and of the voluntary and federal Europe, based on mutual economic advantage and the elimination of the capacity of nation–states to make war, which is being constructed today, nearly two centuries later. The Emperor's formula which most clearly foreshadowed present federal ideas was the one he used during a visit to Charlemagne's capital of Aachen in 1805: 'There will be no peace in Europe until the whole continent is under one suzerain.' President Mitterand in his farewell address to the European Parliament at Strasbourg echoed this idea. He declared that the alternative to the European Union 'is nationalism and war'.

The Sponge option

The second alternative was what the Anglo-Hanoverian Heeren had in mind when in his history of the European states system written during the Napoleonic wars he described the Holy Roman Empire as a sponge, useful to all and dangerous to none, and able to absorb the increasing pressures generated by the states system.[5] Heeren, and those who saw the grande république more or less as he did, wanted central Europe to continue to fulfil its function as a multilateral shock absorber.

Instead of uniting the German states and statelets in an imperial Europe, the sponge alternative would have left the centre of the continent fragmented in a Europe of multiple independences, but would have given every major European power a say in the affairs of a reconstituted Holy Roman Empire.[6] From today's perspective we can see that the complex institution of the Empire was, as Voltaire observed, '*ni saint, ni empire, ni romain*'; but also that Heeren was justified in calling it useful to all, which few Europeans recognized in the age of nationalism. James Sheehan has recently formulated concisely its relevance to our discussion:

> The Reich came from a historical world in which nationality had no political meaning, and states did not command total sovereignty. Unlike nations and states, the Reich did not insist on pre-eminent authority and unquestioning allegiance. Its goal was not to clarify and dominate, but rather to order and balance fragmented institutions and multiple loyalties.[7]

There is an unmistakeable family resemblance between the Empire and today's European Union.

An arrangement of that kind might seem superficially like the 1945 division of Germany into four zones, each occupied by a great power. But Heeren's concept of a sponge was not at all like the conquest and partition of a national state by its enemies. It was rather the linking of the great powers of Europe in the constituent authority of an area that had for centuries consisted of a number of autonomous states held together in a confederal Roman Reich. The sponge formula did not offer Napoleon's social reforms and economic integration to the dynamic classes of Europe, but it would have involved all the great powers more actively in central Europe than did the more national

Deutsche Bund or German Confederation set up by the Vienna settlement, and would have mitigated the forthcoming concentration of power in a national German state. To that extent it would have imposed greater limits on the freedom of action of the members of the European society of states, and moved it further along the spectrum towards supranational authority than the Concert of Europe after 1815 was able to do.

Both these solutions to the future German problem, if we may call them that, would have been pre-emptive. It is a lot to expect statesmen, preoccupied with immediate problems, to anticipate those which have not yet appeared over the horizon.

The Austrian option

The third range of alternatives falls between the other two and most resembles the Vienna settlement. That settlement accorded Austria an unquestioned primacy in the confederation that replaced the former Holy Roman Empire. Austria, the heir of the Empire, could have taken the lead in organizing the *Zollverein* or economic integration of the confederation around itself, while leaving the legitimate sovereigns in place as a mosaic of political autonomies. The Austrian imperial government had the opportunity to bring the area between the Rhine and the Oder into a larger union with the wide Danubian area on the other side of Vienna, much of which Austria had recently reconquered from the Ottomans. In fact Metternich's Austria was too conservative, too indifferent to economics and too defensive to undertake the task.

Moreover Austria's defensive position both in Germany and in Italy, based on a network of client states, had for some time been a necessary condition of the similar French influence in those two areas, and thus of a balance in Europe.[8] Madame de Pompadour and the Empress Maria Theresa saw this more clearly in the eighteenth century[9] than Napoleon III in the nineteenth. He blithely encouraged nationalism in Italy and opposed Austria. His policy helped to open the way first for a united Italy, which excluded French influence there also, and then for the troisième Allemagne to unite with Prussia in a German nation state, and so for the German problem to take the form it did.

In the age of nationalism, progressive opinion demanded that every Volk should have an independent state through which to realise its destiny. The Austrian and Ottoman empires in particular were regarded as anachronisms. Austria was labelled 'a prison of nationalities'. But the Habsburgs had managed to bring together round the spinal cord of the Danube an area that had considerable geographic and economic coherence. The same was true of the Ottoman empire, which held together an area with a millenial tradition of coherence imparted by its Byzantine predecessor. The regimes associated with Metternich and the Ottoman Sultans were indeed oppressive and unpopular. Only recently have people like myself begun to see that they also had advantages, and that in rejecting Metternich's management of Europe so absolutely we may have thrown the baby out with the bath water. Now that the ideal of the independent wilful nation–state is beginning to fade in Europe, and the Danubian states aspire to merge their sovereignties in the European Union, we are more prepared to consider the merits of alternative solutions to the problems of the Austrian and Ottoman imperial states, rather than simply to assume that disintegration was inevitable.

INDUSTRIALIZATION

Part of the difficulty was that the industrialization of Europe proceeded on national lines within the hide of each great leviathan state. The industrial revolution made untrammeled nation–states more dangerous and more capable of vast destruction. Industrialization and the development of what we might call a modern economy came rather later to central Europe than to Britain, where the industrial revolution began. The piecemeal development of the German *Zollverein* or free trade area from 1828 united two of the three Germanies into a single economic entity; the creation of the second Reich in 1871 united them into the premier political and military power in Europe. In the new German Reich and elsewhere industrialization was fostered and developed largely by the state itself.

The great increase of industrial and economic power was largely produced by the classes most passionately committed to nationalism, so that the logic of industrial development and the aspiration of national unity led Germans in the same direction, as it led Italians and others. By contrast in the Austro-Hungarian empire, excluded from the new Germany and the new Italy but allied to them, industrialization and the rise of an influential middle class proceeded more slowly, and at odds with linguistic nationalism. Nevertheless the realized and potential development of the Danubian area increased the pressures engendered by the general industrialization of Europe. Industrial development in Germany and Austria–Hungary began to grow to an extent and at a rate which upset the balance. The Germans saw themselves as a *Volk ohne Raum*, but there was not enough room in Europe to absorb the increasing pressures of the continent's industrialized nation–states. The collective hegemony of the European concert had been weakened, and the rest of Europe began to feel threatened by the hegemony of a single power, the new German Reich.

The political union of Prussia and the *troisième Allemagne* was brought about by Bismarck, who belonged to the pre-industrial Prussia east of the Elbe. Bismarck distrusted pan-German nationalism: for him the new Reich, insofar as it was Prussia writ large, was a satiated power. To protect Prussia's achievement he wanted to create a firm order in Europe. European order had been based on a consensus of great powers achieved through congresses. Bismarck maintained collective hegemony for extra-European problems, but abandoned it in Europe, preferring to rely on voluntary self-limitation by each individual great power. His order was held in place by a satisfied Germany in tacit partnership with Britain and Russia, the two great 'bookend' powers which wanted peace in Europe and might help him exercise the restraint he knew was necessary. He therefore opposed Germany acquiring overseas colonies or an ocean-going navy capable of challenging Britannia's rule of the waves, and maintained cordial relations with Russia too. He also regretted the decision to take Alsace and Lorraine 'back' from France, which fatally embittered relations with that country.

Bismarck did not aim at German hegemony. He relied on a complex balance of multiple independences, which he managed with political genius. So long as he conducted the foreign relations of the new German state and dominated those of most of Europe, the incipient German hegemony remained acceptable. The flaw in his order, it seems to me with the benefit of hindsight, was that he moved the practice of the *grande république* significantly further towards the anarchic end of the spectrum just when industrialization was tightening the net that pressed the states of Europe more closely against each other.

Bismarck's order gave Europe twenty years of peace. But after his dismissal in 1890 a new Germany asserted itself, with sources of strength released by unification and military success, in the same general way as the revolution had enabled France to realize her full potential a hundred years before. The Germans seemed to be taking the lead in industry and science as well as military efficiency.[10] The statistics of steel production, armaments and so forth are impressive; but what struck contemporaries even more were the organizational efficiency and commitment of the Germans. Europeans then accepted that they lived in an increasingly competitive world of the survival of the fittest independent states. They also recognized that the power of a state was determined not only by its economic and technological capacity and its political organization, which in central Europe had been transformed by the gradual gathering together of the second Reich, but also and especially, as Barnett puts it, by 'the people; their skills, energy, ambition, discipline, initiatives; their beliefs, myths and illusions'.[11]

The increase in Germany's strength relative to her neighbours was eminently legitimate. The new Reich did nothing contrary to the lax rules of the society, and in particular it did not attack or threaten to attack any other European state. Breaking off the reinsurance treaty with Russia, or building a navy to match Britain's, or the new Kaiser's ostentatious visit to the Ottoman Empire were highly imprudent, and the government of the Reich behaved with a certain arrogance and tactlessness which caused annoyance to other governments and deeper resentment among their publics. Such actions could be called irresponsible, but no law or code of conduct ruled against them.

In the decades before the First World War, the era of imperialism outside Europe, nationalist Germans argued that the other great European powers, Britain, Russia and France, could establish extra-European empires powerful enough to counterbalance and make acceptable a German continental hegemony. In any case a German hegemony would be much looser than French dominion under the Napoleonic formula. But in the age of powerful sovereign nation states jostling for room in a Europe too small for them, a number of other states were unwilling to accept a German hegemony. What alarmed the rest of Europe was not imprudent German actions in themselves, but the steady and apparently inexorable increase in the relative power of the German state in an international society that had no effective means of restraining it except an anti-hegemonial alliance. The tsarist autocracy of Russia and the French republic were also animated by nationalist passions, which in France took the form of a chauvinistic desire for revenge. Russia and France looked on each other with antipathy; but first they, and then Britain that had been traditionally hostile to both, came together in an anti-hegemonial coalition[12] to preserve the only restraint which the European society then respected, the balance of power.

These pressures generated at the same time an emotional popular germanophobia in the neighbours of the new Reich and indeed throughout the *grande république*. In that age of nationalist passion, popular germanophobia was like anti-semitism, based largely on envy and fear of perceived German economic and intellectual eminence.

Indeed the most anti-German Frenchmen were also the most anti-semitic.

So the restraints finally broke, and let slip the dogs of war. This was not to be another of the painful but tolerable wars of adjustment familiar to the statesmen, the armed services and the general publics of Europe. What began in 1914 with a fizz of nationalist enthusiasm was a catastrophe of unforeseen and perhaps unforeseeable magnitude.[13]

THE PROBLEM AFTER WORLD WAR I

The question raised by the existence of a large and industrially efficient German state in the middle of an anarchically organized Europe was temporarily eased but certainly not solved by the First World War.

After that war the United States found itself the world's strongest power. Under President Wilson's[14] leadership the principal victor powers decided to implement nationalist aspirations in Europe in accordance with democracy and sovereignty by means of **self-determination**.[15] There are grave objections of principle to this approach. If you accept the proposition, then general in Europe, that there are nations or Völker distinct from states, and that every nation has a right to an independent state, it may seem simple and democratic to find out which nation the people of a given area belong to and which state they therefore wish to have govern them. But in fact populations are mixed and loyalties divided, and the difficulties of minorities in nation–states are great.

The exasperated and war-shocked victor statesmen applied the principle arbitrarily and injudiciously in Europe, and occasionally ignored the result of their public consultations. They provided a grand example of Simone Weil's memorable phrase 'Justice, that fugitive from the victors' camp'. The Ottoman empire was divided up even more arbitrarily and with little consultation of the population, largely into dependent mandates of the great powers who undertook to bring the new 'nations' to independence as soon as practicable.[16] The result was to balkanize or to recognize the balkanization of the whole great area between Switzerland and Persia. That proliferation of many small states, all granted or promised independence, brought a further element of instability and suffering to the area, from which it has not yet recovered.

The First World War weakened and humiliated Germany, but left it still potentially the strongest and most energetic state in Europe. A virtual power vacuum in the balkanized area to its east was incapable of exercising any serious restraint on it. The war had weakened Britain and France about as much, though less visibly. Russia had become the Soviet Union, like Germany another war-ruined pariah cut off from the West.

The destruction of the old order in Europe opened up three possible ways of coping with the concentration of power in an independent Germany. The first was to set limits to independence in Europe by creating a genuine supranational authority: for instance, a collective hegemony of all the major powers, including Germany. The collective authority would need to be at least as effective in limiting independence as the concert of great powers after the defeat of Napoleon. The second option was to break up the new German Reich, and especially the concentration of economic power in the west of the state, in a manner likely to have some permanence. The third option was to revert to a Europe of multiple independences and to grant the Weimar Republic full sovereignty and a position commensurate with its capacities in an anarchic Europe. Each of the three solutions was beset by great difficulties.

The trouble with the first solution, a **genuine supranational authority** in Europe, is that it would have obliged the European victor powers to relinquish a substantial degree of their own sovereignty. This they were not then willing to do. The United States was not prepared even to consider taking such a course. It was not that the Western victors failed to recognize the dangers of international anarchy. They, and especially President Wilson, did see the problem. But the measures of 'collective security' that they agreed on were weak and voluntary. The allied leaders were also too anti-hegemonial, and too committed to independence, to produce an adequate supranational authority. Sovereign independence remained the constituent principle of the Versailles settlement and the League of Nations, and indeed the victors were willing to foster nationalism by abolishing empires in favour of so-called nation–states.

The founders of the League thought that the dangers of international anarchy could be overcome by separating the two basic claims of sovereigns: restricting their external freedom of action on the one hand, but permitting and indeed protecting their domestic independence on the other. The League relied on what is sometimes called solidarism[17] to ensure that its good and responsible member states would honour their perpetual covenant to prevent an 'aggressor' (meaning essentially Germany) from altering the new order by force. Whether solidarism would have worked for long even if all the other major powers had been actively willing to support an unsatisfactory *status quo* (for that is what it amounted to) is very doubtful. But the four greatest concentrations of power in the twentieth century – the United States, Russia, and Japan as well as Germany – were all absent from the League or indifferent to solidarism. The abstention of the greatest powers, and thus of an effective collective hegemony, left the covenant quite inadequate to the burden it assumed. On balance there was a shift along the spectrum away from absolute independences, but a small one.

The second solution, the forcible **breakup of Germany,** was blocked by equally great difficulties. It would mean the denial of democracy and self-determination to Germans. More demandingly, it would mean prolonged military occupation of the successor states and the enforcement of barriers to economic co-operation between them until their publics came to accept partition, if they ever did. The Western victors were altogether unwilling to enforce such draconian and long-term measures on their own, or to enlist the help of Bolshevik Russia. Though such a plan seemed farfetched, it bears some resemblance to what the victors discussed after World War II, and even began to put into practice.

The third solution was to accept a **German say** in a Europe of multiple independences, commensurate with that country's formidable strength and abilities. This solution would have probably ensued if the war had been brought to an end before the collapse of Russia and the defeat of Germany. After the defeat of Napoleon the victors at the Vienna settlement had been willing to co-opt France on that basis. The Weimar Republic appeared to be a reformed social-democratic state. Even so in 1919 this solution was emotionally the least acceptable of the three to the European victors, especially to public opinion in western Europe in its post-war mood of bitterness.

Six years later it seemed for a moment that the western allies might accept the Germans as equal partners. The Locarno agreement of 1925 with Britain and France, which guaranteed the new western frontiers but left the eastern ones open, and which gave Weimar Germany a great-power permanent seat at the League Council, seemed the first step. But the European states remained sovereign and independent. Given the disintegration of Eastern Europe, a commensurate say would soon put the Germans in a more hegemonial position than ever, which was precisely what the allies had fought the war to avoid. The promise of Locarno soon faded.

So in fact the Versailles settlement achieved none of the three solutions. It neither established an adequate supranational authority, nor broke up the concentration of power in a united German state, nor offered the Germans equal rights (*Gleichberechtigung*) and a place among the great powers corresponding to their strength. The delegates of the victor powers returning home from the peace conference were already depressed by a sense of failure.[18] Their forebodings turned out to be dismally true.

The **options for the German state** after the First World War are also instructive, and foreshadow the courses followed by the two halves of Germany after the second. Once it was clear that Germany would remain independent and united, the Weimar republic set about mending its relations with both the West and Russia. The Locarno agreement accepted the new German frontiers in the west, while the Rapallo agreement opened the way for German–Soviet economic collaboration and the training of German military cadres in Russia. The Weimar concept of Germany seemed to be an independent national state, with a limited defensive capacity and territorially restricted.[19] It would earn its way in the world by exporting industrial and technological goods and importing food and raw materials.

Converting Weimar Germany into what Professor Calleo[20] calls an export–import machine was a plausible option. West Germany and Japan have done it successfully since World War II. But it meant making Germany's livelihood dependent on the goodwill of what many Germans saw, with some justification, as a hostile world – in other words accepting stringent economic limits on its freedom of action, to which for instance Britain with its empire was not subjected. Hitler and his followers rejected this formula. They intended to have an independent state with untrammeled freedom of action. Remembering the food shortages during the war and the subsequent blockade, they wanted a German Reich able to feed itself in wartime. Before the recent agrarian revolution self-sufficiency in food meant acquiring more territory in the east, where the Nazis planned to settle Germans in place of the inhabitants.

Americans saw more clearly than Germany's European neighbours the need to encourage the economic revival of the Weimar Republic to ensure moderation in Germany and to help Europe recover from the ruin of the war, and they began to act on their perception. But the great economic depression which occurred ten years after the war destroyed the Weimar regime and brought Hitler to power.

As German strength recovered in an atmosphere of autarchy and rearmament, the other major European states looked again at the options they had not taken up at Versailles. The flimsy restraints of the League of Nations did not prevent international society from becoming looser and more anarchic than ever. Laval of France, who preferred expediency to principle, tried to forge an old-fashioned, anti-hegemonial coalition with Britain, Fascist Italy and the Communist Soviet Union to restrain Germany, but when this failed he tried to save French interests by collaborating with a hegemonial Germany under Hitler. Stalin soon reached the same conclusion. In Britain Chamberlain tried to strike a bargain that would appease Hitler's publicly stated ambitions in Europe and keep the British imperial structure in place. Hitler thought the way was open for his eastern adventure. But when he embarked on it Britain and France declared war, and so wrenched the struggle round from the east of Germany to the west.

The First World War was essentially a struggle between European states fired by nationalist passion, with little of the ideological content that had marked the wars of the French Revolution or the religious wars. The point has often been made that if, during the abortive American attempt to negotiate a peace in 1916, either side had agreed to the inflated war demands of the other, that side would nevertheless have been better off than it was at the end of the war. For the allies a negotiated peace brokered by the Americans would have meant accepting a greater degree of German hegemony in Europe. In retrospect that hardly seems as unacceptable as it did in the days of war fever. The first war quickly came to seem senseless to most Europeans. The war against Hitler was much more ideological and indeed ethical, especially for the United States; it is difficult to see how a compromise with him could have been negotiated. But the war between Japan and America was nationalist rather than ideological, more like the First World War in Europe.

ANARCHOPHOBIA, OR EUROPEAN UNION

One purpose of Hitler's brief and tyrannical occupation of Europe was to harness the rest of the continent to the Nazi-controlled ideological war machine. Napoleon had a similar purpose. He insisted on the primacy of France, but he also introduced ideas and methods that had general validity, and opened up opportunities to the rising middle class in other countries. By contrast, Hitler's occupation offered few advantages to non-Germans and was made especially odious by such monstrous acts as the holocaust of Jews and others. Even so, many of Hitler's enemies were impressed by the advantages which a unified European economy brought to the Nazi war effort.

The Second World War further inflamed nationalist passions. But this time the passions turned sour. A second disastrous war, coming so closely on the heels of the first, bred an awareness in Europe, and especially in Germany, that the structure of international society itself was woefully inadequate, and that the concentration of virtually unlimited sovereignty in the hands of nation–states was too dangerous. Most Europeans today no longer regard the claims of linguistic nationalism and Wilsonian self-determination as self evident, or even desirable. Rather the horrifying practical consequences of these claims have inseminated into men's minds a certain fear of limitless national independence.

In World War II the Kreisau group of Prussian men and women considered it their duty as individuals, as Germans and as Europeans to assassinate Hitler. They formulated the truly remarkable insight in time of war that the potential of a cultural or political entity (such as Germany) can be realized only if some supranational structure is able to restrain the tendencies which Hitler personified.

> The free and peaceful development of national culture can no longer go hand in hand with the maintenance of the absolute sovereignty of individual states. Peace requires the individual states to be included in an overarching order. As soon as all the peoples concerned have freely agreed, the supporters of this order must have the right to ask every individual to obey and respect the highest political authority of the community of peoples, and also in cases of need to commit his or her life and property to it.[21]

The overarching order demanded by the document anticipates a European Union and looks back to the Holy Roman Empire. Particularly significant is the conviction that the absolute independence of states is incompatible with the free development of national cultures. It takes anarchophobia beyond the fear of war. The Kreisau group feared the stultifying effect of untrammeled nationalism on civilization in peacetime as well; for them National Socialism was the worst but not the only example.

On a much wider scale the Nazi conquest and domination of continental Europe also moved a large and dynamic section of European opinion there, led in the West by men like Monnet, Schumann, de Gasperi and Adenauer, to want a united Europe substantially further along the spectrum away from the multiple independences that had proved so disastrous. The British were more committed to independence, but Churchill too echoed the spirit of the time: 'We shall only save ourselves from the perils which draw near by forgetting the hatreds of the past . . . by progressively effacing frontiers and barriers which aggravate and congeal our divisions.'[22]

Europeans who held these opinions wanted the change on two main counts. First, Hitler's ability to arm Germany and unleash a war made it seem essential to overcome the perils of nationalist and sovereign anarchy if Europe was to survive. The war-making capacity of European states must be integrated into a **supranational structure** firm enough to resist the dictates of a single member state. Second, we saw that even so detested a regime as Hitler's opened the eyes of many Europeans to the material advantages of the **economic integration** of Europe. The European federalists (and many others too) wanted to perpetuate those advantages by means of free negotiation, provided they could ensure that the unified European economy would not be dominated by any one nation–state, especially Germany.

The sense that the benefits of a European Union or confederacy outweigh the disadvantages is the current European form of anarchophobia. Federalists consider the surrender of national sovereignty not a price to be paid for union, but the positive advantage which union will bring. In their eyes the principal function of a democratic European community or confederal union is to establish collective control of foreign policy and defence, and so to take away from nation states the external aspects of sovereignty, such as the ability to make war. The benefits of economic and monetary union are secondary; but they are real, and achievable. And indeed that is where the most significant integration has so far been realized. Once these goals are accepted, it is not a large step to let the Union determine some of the internal political practices of its members as well. The Union which the federalists seek involves the gradual but steady surrender of the freedom of action of its once independent member states, externally and internally, until they become little more than autonomous provinces ceremonially still dressed in the trappings of sovereignty.

From the beginning the **military** aspects of supranational security had a wider dimension than Europe. The hot war against Hitler and the cold war against Stalin both required American resources and therefore American leadership. During the cold war the armed forces of Western Europe, including West Germany, were integrated in NATO under American command. NATO is an alliance not a confederation, but it and the integration of the West European iron and steel industry put real curbs on the military independence of the West European states, and made acceptable a substantial West German contribution to the common defence. In the military field, which is what mattered most to the federalists, NATO did much of their work for them.

Economic and political integration were more specifically confined to western Europe, and political integration largely to the area occupied by the Nazis. The lacerated western half of Europe was confronted by two realities. The first was the absence of a peace settlement, so that it was necessary to improvise a substitute. The second reality was the cold war and the partition of the continent along the iron curtain. In particular only West Germany, the former *troisième Allemagne*, was available to the West. The Rhinelander Adenauer was determined to make his part of Germany acceptable to the Western powers, and especially to build on its traditional links with France to achieve an integrated Western Europe.

So it was that after Hitler's overthrow the six countries on the west of the iron curtain that had been most affected by Nazi control – France, West Germany, Italy and the Benelux states – never wholly undid their compulsory integration. Animated by anarchophobe reaction against sovereign independences, they started down the road leading to voluntary political federation by establishing the European Community through the Treaty of Rome in 1958. In the west the momentum of the six brought in other European states.

Whereas Britain and France have been organized for centuries as what we now call nation–states, the allegiances and administrative structures of Central Europe have changed several times in the fairly recent past. In a historical atlas the map of Central Europe alters every few years like a kaleidoscope.[23] Consequently it is not as difficult for the Central Europeans as it is for the British and French to consider alternatives to a Europe of independent nation–states; and it will be less difficult for them to transfer some major administrative functions, and also some of their sense of identity, from a virtually exclusive focus on independent states to a larger community, the European Union. The smaller peoples of the area – Hungarians, Czechs, Slovenes – equally want to merge some aspects of their sovereignty in a wider political federation. Such diffused attachments are what Sheehan described in the passage quoted above as the goal of the Holy Roman Empire: 'to order and balance fragmented institutions and multiple loyalties'.

The aims of the West European federalists were made more acceptable by the decline of Europe from being the centre and determining area of international society to being only one area among many in a more integrated global system, which during the cold war was dominated by the United Sates and Russia. A federation would, the federalists argue, restore some of Europe's diminished economic and perhaps political clout in the world.

Measures of supranational economic regulation such as a common currency, open markets and free trade, and standardization of commercial law and weights and measures, bring considerable economic benefits at the price of short-term dislocation. Such benefits do not need a political union: most of them can be obtained in a free trade area or *Zollverein*. That was not enough for those who favoured a supranational authority to overcome the dangers of independent nation–states. But it seemed far enough along the road to integration for Britain and some other European states grouped in the European Free Trade Area. Non-Communist Europe appeared to be divided for a time into two blocs. In fact the disagreement between federalists and sceptics cut and still cuts across national boundaries.

Europe east of the iron curtain, including Eastern Germany, was similarly integrated under Soviet occupation. Defence and economic life were firmly in Soviet hands. The Soviets effected a degree of political integration through local communist parties, but the outward façade of independent statehood was kept in place. Adenauer's counterpart in Eastern Germany, Ulbricht, was equally determined to make his territory comply with the wishes of the dominant power, and the so-called Democratic Republic was the most docile of the Soviet satellites. The peoples of Eastern Europe ardently wanted to be free from the alien, corrupt and inefficient Soviet occupation. It is evidence of the change in European political thinking since the Second World War, that following their liberation from Soviet and communist domination they do not now want to revert to a dangerous independence, but look forward to a confederal association with Western Europe. The reunification of the two Germanies and the subsequent disintegration of the Soviet Union have increased the attractive power of the two institutions which promote European integration: the European Union and the NATO alliance. Both are now in the slow and difficult process of eastern enlargement.

Even so, as the integration progresses it steps on many toes. Inevitably national sentiment and damaged vested interests produce considerable opposition. When pendulums swing, their momentum carries them further than the optimum point. A crusade produces a reaction. Opposition is strongest in Britain, where a long anti-hegemonial tradition (described in the next chapter) was reinforced by the bitter and damaging struggle to preserve independence in the Second World War. In particular, the European Union needs to be careful not to disturb more than is necessary the institutions and symbols of sovereignty round which the loyalties of most Europeans have crystallized.

The German **economy** is now conspicuously the strongest in the European Union, and gives Germany, insofar as it remains a nation–state, a hegemonial position there. Germans naturally want to develop their economic capacities to the full. It is in the interest of all Europe that they should do so. But most Germans are ashamed of the Nazi abuse of unrestricted national power both outside and inside Germany, and dismayed by the continuing resentment of the victims. They see, or sense, that if their full potential is to be acceptable to their neighbours, it must be developed within a wider framework. The whole economy of the Union must follow the example of the iron, coal and steel community, and emancipate itself from control by national governments. Fortunately for those who want a more effective Union, many European private enterprises are moving quite rapidly in this direction in their competitive search for profitability.

For the same reasons the **military** contribution of united Germany, the largest in Europe, must also remain integrated in a wider structure. American predominance in the defence framework of NATO, while it lasts, gives the US the ability to block unilateral German action. But the American commitment to keep large forces in non-communist Europe may continue to weaken, in the absence of a threat from the East and as a result of the growing American preoccupation with domestic problems. An integrated European defence force will gradually take shape as a logical corollary of European Union.

The **cultural** dimension of European Union is rarely discussed in public. Yet Europe is as much a cultural as a geographical concept: it is still a slightly enlarged *grande république*. The dynamic culture and civilization of Europe owes its vigour to diversity rather than to sameness. If the diverse elements of Europe are to nourish each other, they must not be insulated from each other within the confines of narrow nationalism; nor on the other hand must they be homogenized. More elastic than de Gaulle's phrase '*l'Europe des patries*' is Helena Vaz da Silva's '*l'Europe des différences*',[24] which recognizes both individuality and membership without insisting on nation–states.

Half a century after the Second World War the supranational structure which the Kreisau Prussians, Monnet and others called for is a familiar idea and is becoming a reality. Its priorities are well epitomized by the French President Mitterand's farewell declaration to the European Parliament at Strasbourg, that the alternative to European Union 'is nationalism and war'. The German Chancellor Helmut Kohl has often said[25] that independent national states are no longer a practicable form of government in Europe, and that European Union means freedom and peace. By this alliterative phrase

(*Freiheit und Frieden*) he means freedom for individual citizens through the limitation of the domestic powers of European states, and, like Mitterand, peace through the effective removal from the states of the ability to make war.

These statesmen and others who share their aim have in mind that the member states of the union should surrender some powers upward, to a supranational confederal authority, the European Union, and others perhaps downward to smaller units or regions. But while the general purpose and nature of the proposed overarching structure are reasonably clear, its practice is not. The confederal authority is not to be a state, or at least not what Europeans have meant by a state in the last two hundred years, or in the sense that India for instance is a multi-ethnic federal state. Yet the frame of the union must be strong enough to impose firm limits on independent action by any member national state, especially the most powerful (at present Germany).

Of the powers to be surrendered by the member states, military capacity and the ability to create military capacity might seem the most important. However, military capacity is no longer the crux of the matter. In practice other Europeans no longer fear military hegemony by Germany, or being dragged by Germany into external military adventures. What germanophobes fear is some kind of economic domination by a Germany that still has enough power at the national level to exercise such control. Emotional fears cannot be exorcized by promises: the checks and balances, the delegation of powers to the overarching authority, must be seen to be fully adequate to prevent domination by the economically strongest state. These anxieties apply particularly to Germany, but also, and perhaps more realistically, to a diarchy of Germany and France. The litmus test of an overarching European authority will be that it, rather than member states, takes major economic and political decisions, and that no one or two states, acting in their own interests, are able to dominate the authority's decisions. To use Napoleon's Aachen formula, all Europe would be brought under one suzerain, but that suzerain would be genuinely collective enough to prevent anything like Napoleon's own domination.

So we come to the crucial practical questions. These are uncharted waters. The practice of the overarching authority will have to proceed experimentally. Statesmen will have to feel their way. Until some experience has been gained, it will be difficult to set out the authority's unfamiliar functions in a formal constitution. Will the member states remain the focus of government and of their citizens' loyalty? Will the supranational collective authority, the European Union, begin by being no more than an effective mechanism for imposing limits on their independence? If so, will the division of administrative responsibilities, and the checks and balances needed to impose effective restraints, paralyse the ability of the Union or its member states to make decisions? Or alternatively, will the need to reach and carry out decisions become so insistent that it pushes the supranational Union quite quickly to become a federal state, with a central government that determines policy in certain major fields? In any case, are the policies of the Union, and its evolving relationship with the member states, likely to be shaped in practice mainly by the two largest members – which means a Franco-German diarchy?

These questions may seem formidable. But the last century of European history bears out Mitterand's and Kohl's strong warnings that to leave the limits of independence as loose as they now are involves graver risks, and that sovereign nation–states have become a dangerous anachronism in Europe.

One of the most interesting aspects of the European Union, as it exists and as it promises to become, is the nature of the hegemonial authority which it is already able to exercise over a wide area. The Danish scholar Ole Waever points out that 'the overarching image is of one centre and concentric circles, a completely different mental geography from the usual one of several competing great powers'. He notes that the European Union exercises a great magnetism in the East of Europe, where the states that wish to join or develop a close association with the European Union make their economic and other policies conform as closely as they can to European Union standards. 'Politicians in these countries have known very well that the eyes of the EC were on them, and they knew what counted as good and bad behaviour (regarding democracy, minorities, privatization and sub-regional relations).' Waever calls this influence 'silent disciplining power on the near abroad'. That is an apt description of hegemonial authority.[26]

THE LESSONS OF INADEQUATE RESTRAINTS

We can draw a number of conclusions from the above perspective of recent European history. The most outstanding is the lesson drawn by the majority of Europeans today, that we need much firmer limits to the freedom of action of European states than existed earlier in this century.

From the failure of Louis XIV to consolidate the ascendancy of France (say 1700) until the unification of Prussia and Western Germany into a nation–state (1870), the European princes were able to manage their relations with remarkably few limits to their independence. There were wars of adjustment, but they did not disturb the progress of European civilization. After 1815 the collective hegemony of the great powers kept Europe in something of a strait-jacket. And there was one exceptional period, when the torrent of martial and other energy released in France by the revolution enabled Napoleon to make his bid for empire. Even so, for most of that century and a half the balance of power, *raison de système*, and a general sense of prudence and responsibility enabled the princes' club to allow its members unusual freedom of action, both externally and internally. That was an impressive achievement. But in the century of the nationalist demos, those largely voluntary restraints were unable to prevent the catastrophe of two great European wars.

From Napoleon's time the organization of Central Europe, the Germanies, has been the pivotal question. In all the alternative ways of organizing Europe, the central issue has been how this key area can be fitted into the *grande république*. Looking back with the rueful hindsight of experience, many in my generation pay special attention to the attempts to incorporate Central Europe into a wider restraining structure. The European Union does seem to provide an answer. But many in Europe (and outside it) wonder whether the Germans can still be regarded as a hegemonial threat. Has their former commitment to national unity through blood and iron given way to a Scandinavian dislike of force? Have the question, and the anxiety, been overtaken by events? Is the question relevant in the new context of a Europe that no longer occupies a central position in the states system?

One aspect of the European tragedy seems clear. Europe in the century from about 1850 to about 1950, with its anarchic international society and its nationalist passions, was unable to achieve the benefits which the gifts and capacities of the Central Europeans could have brought to the whole, if the Germans in particular had been able to develop their talents without being compressed into an explosive force. Parallel with that loss was the diversion of a great part of the capacities and emotions of other European peoples from constructive achievement to the *Einkreisung* or bottling up of the German national state.

Second in importance to the position of the Germanies in the organization of Europe is the role of France. French statesmen and scholars have traditionally thought of Europe in terms of hegemony. For centuries before the 1860s France, unlike the Germanies, was a single effective state, at least the equal of any in Europe; and the other powers acknowledged its indispensable part in the organization of the *grande république*. After that France began to fall behind Britain and Germany in population and industrial capacity, and Napoleon III's unwise policies cost it the leadership in Europe, but it was still able to animate an anti-hegemonial coalition against Germany. Exhausted and embittered by the First World War, the French failed to establish a working co-operation with the Weimar Republic. But it seems to me that they have learnt well the bitter lessons of that failure and the Hitler period. French realism and statesmanship towards the Germanies since de Gaulle and Adenauer knelt together in Reims Cathedral has made possible the European Community and Union. The European Union already has a hegemonial position in Europe. Until some or all of the states which compose it merge a substantial part of their individual sovereignties under a supranational 'political roof', it is being managed by a hegemony of its two most powerful members, the 'Paris–Bonn axis'. A shared hegemony is an acceptable compromise for the French, so long as it remains more or less in balance. But a hegemonial diarchy has always proved to be an uneasy relationship.

Difficulties of the opposite kind affect the role of the two great powers on the margins of Europe. In the nineteenth century Europe was the dominant centre of the worldwide system, and a single imperial or even hegemonial power there would dominate the whole. The traditional opposition of both Britain and Russia, the two 'book-end powers' of Europe, made it difficult and in the long run impossible for a continental hegemony or dominion to consolidate and gain legitimacy. But both Britain and Russia understood that the alternative form of order, a stable balance of power, required their active participation in the European concert, and both fairly consistently used their influence to promote the doctrine of independence coupled with the practice of restraint. During the course of the twentieth century the United States has effectively replaced Britain as the great power to the west of Europe. In the last fifty years it has played a more active role in European affairs, and particularly in Germany, than Britain usually did in previous times. In a sense the US and the Soviet Union continued to act as bookend powers. By pushing against one another they kept Europe for forty years in a state of immobile order.

The British people, who until recently saw themselves as the creators and animators of an extra-European worldwide empire, are now somewhat bewildered about their relation to the rest of the world. The American Secretary of State Dean Acheson said unkindly of Britain that it had lost an empire and had not yet found another role. The British did not lose their empire so much as actively divest themselves of it; many of them look back on it with an unhistorical sense of unease or guilt. Britain played a pivotal role in NATO, which organized the defence of Western Europe against the Soviet Union, and also provided the machinery for integrating both US and West German military capacity into a supranational defence structure. But it seems to me that since the Second World War British political leaders, and the public, have been less perceptive and less statesmanlike than their French counterparts in dealing with other aspects of their involvement in Europe, and in developing a working partnership with the Germans in particular. Yet the British have traditionally shown a knack for pragmatic adaptation of rules in the light of experience, and the European Union, which is long on theory and short on practice, will need this knack.

Europe too has shrunk to being merely one part of the worldwide system which the Europeans created. A confederacy which embraced the whole of Europe would be a major power in the global system and of international society, but still only one player among many. The larger system itself might remain loosely co-ordinated, as it now is, or it might revert to an anarchy of multiple independences. In either such system there would remain the problem of an imbalance of power. This is not a problem that the Europeans can now solve for themselves. Perhaps nothing short of a wider supranational hegemonial authority or partnership for peace, including the United States, a European Union, Russia and the major Asian states, is the minimum now required to provide convincing limits to the freedom of action of great concentrations of power.

NOTES

1 A degree of order was maintained first by the pressures and constraints of the system itself – the fact of the close involvement of the political entities with each other – which the states so involved found it too dangerous or unrewarding to disregard. Second, the states involved in the system regulated these pressures by voluntary agreements between themselves, including individual alliances and the general rules and institutions of the European international society. Third, an additional degree of order was negotiated and imposed by the hegemonial authority of one or more

great powers. Wight in a much-quoted phrase described the European society as a succession of hegemonies, and my *Evolution of International Society* argues that hegemony is an integral and inevitable characteristic of all societies of states that can be described as close to the anarchic or multiple independences end of the spectrum.

2 Oswald Spengler, *Der Untergang des Abendlandes*, Beck Munich 1922, vol. 2, p. 132. My translation. This passage was denounced in 1932 by Joseph Goebbels as contrary to National Socialism. On that point Dr Goebbels was undoubtedly right.

3 Connelly, *Napoleon's Satellite Kingdoms*, Macmillan, New York, 1965, p. 333.

4 Napoleon's bid to reorganize Europe politically and economically round a French empire was facilitated by the pervasive influence of French civilization on the educated classes of Germany and Italy, and by their familiarity with the French language and openness to French ideas. There was also a significant French immigration into the Germanies, especially by Huguenots. At the beginning of the eighteenth century half of the population of Berlin was French. The philosopher Leibnitz wrote that after the havoc caused in Germany by the Thirty Years' War,

> Nothing could withstand the power of France and the language of France. Our young people . . . who admired everything French, took a dislike to their own language. Many of them entered high positions and posts and thus governed [the many states of] Germany for a long time; and if they did not make it a tributary of French power, they came very near to doing so. In any case they subjected it almost completely to the language, customs and fashions of the French nation.

See R. Hatton, editor, *Louis XIV and Europe*, Macmillan 1976, p. 73. The Germans have had the advantage of such a cultural radiation to a much more limited extent, chiefly in the Danube basin.

5 The powers that generated these pressures included the slowly declining Ottoman empire, which stood outside the European *grande république* but involved the European powers as much by its weakness as previously by its strength, and the Russian empire which was culturally and socially still only a marginal member of the *grande république* but played a major part in the functioning of the society.

6 Austria, Prussia and Britain through Hanover already held electorships. France and Russia would be given similar fiefs (Russia perhaps through Anhalt-Zerbst, which was ruled by Catherine the Great's family). The powers of the electoral princes would have had to be considerably strengthened.

7 James Sheehan, *German History 1770–1866*, Oxford University Press 1989. Emphasis mine.

8 The variable balance between the French and Austrian systems of client princes, bishops and republics in Germany was one aspect of what Heeren meant by the sponge. The two imperial systems legitimized and also neutralized each other.

9 The two powerful and realistic women agreed to defend together the positions and influence which Austria and France had built up in the small states of Germany, Italy and the Low Countries, instead of continuing

to weaken each other as they had hitherto done. The Habsburg Empress Maria Theresa wrote to Louis XV's mistress as *'ma très chère soeur'*.

10 The statistics of steel production, armaments and so forth are impressive. The statistics are conveniently marshalled in Professor Paul Kennedy's *Rise & Fall of the Great Powers*, Random House 1987, especially Chapter 5.

11 Introduction to *Collapse of British Power*, 1972, also quoted by Kennedy, *Rise & Fall of the Great Powers*.

12 The best account of the formation of the Franco-Russian alliance that I know is George Kennan's *The Fateful Alliance*, Pantheon, New York 1984. Kennan's extensive research in the Russian archives documents the nature and extent of germanophobia in St Petersburg.

13 Some moderate statesman foresaw the disaster. The British Foreign Legion Secretary, Sir Edward Grey, declared as the fighting began: 'The lamps are going out all over Europe. We shall not see them lit again in our lifetime.'

14 Wilson has been depicted as a dreamy idealist who suffered from the general American conviction that he understood Europe's problems better than the Europeans, and whose grandiose plan for a League of Nations was not even formulated in terms acceptable to his own legislature. These charges have some validity. But looked at from today's perspective, Wilson appears as more farsighted than the other leading peacemakers at Versailles, and as having a more perceptive diagnosis of the ills of the international society, and a clearer vision of the requirements of international order and especially the responsibilities of the strongest powers.

15 There was much dissent from the principle of self-determination in the delegations of the victor powers at Versailles. For instance Lansing, the American Secretary of State, said 'It will raise hopes which can never be realized. It will I fear cost thousands of lives. . . . In the end it is bound to be discredited, to be called the dream of an idealist who failed to realize the danger until too late to check those who attempt to put the principle in force. What a calamity that the phrase was ever uttered. What misery it will cause.' (Robert Lansing, *The Peace Negotiations* 1921, pp. 97–8.) Lloyd George, in a Memorandum to the conference dated 25 March 1919, said, 'I am . . . strongly averse to transferring more Germans from German rule to the rule of some other state than can possibly be helped.' See also Alfred Cobban, *National Self-determination*, Oxford University Press 1945.

16 See for instance the first chapter of Avi Shlaim's *War and Peace in the Middle East*, Penguin Books 1994. The chapter, entitled *The Post-Ottoman Syndrome*, begins with the sentence 'The Ottoman Empire did not simply decline and disintegrate from within; it was destroyed from without.'

17 On solidarism see Hedley Bull, *The Anarchical Society*, Macmillan, 1977, especially pp. 238–240.

18 The brooding sense of failure is well conveyed, for example, in two farsighted books by members of the British delegation to the Versailles settlement: Harold Nicolson's *Peacemaking 1919* and Maynard Keynes' *The Economic Consequences of the Peace*.

19 The Weimar Republic had revisionist claims in the East, but they were minor and to be agreed with the Western powers.

20 David Calleo, *The German Problem Reconsidered*, Cambridge University Press 1978, pp. 88–89.

21 Marion Grafin Dönhoff, *Um der Ehre Willen*, Siedler 1994. My translation. The operative sentence reads in the original: '*Der Friede erfordert die Schaffung einer der einzelnen Staaten umfassende Ordnung*'.

22 Speech at the Hague Congress of Europe, 7 May 1948.

23 Throughout central Europe administration, economic activity and loyalties have sometimes been spread between a multi-state imperial structure like the Deutsche Bund or Austria–Hungary on the one hand, and a more local entity on the other. Many of the local entities, such as Bavaria, Hamburg, Rome, Hungary or 'the lands of the Czech crown' are at the moment, or were at various recent times, sovereign states. As for the Germans, the Second Reich, the Weimar Republic and the Nazi Third Reich had three different frontiers, constitutions, ideologies and flags. Even if they are taken together, they made a militarily and politically independent nation–state only from 1871 to 1945. Many Germans have come to consider that unstable 74 year experiment to be a failure, or at least now an anachronism.

24 At the time of writing, Senhora Vaz da Silva is the Director of the Portuguese Centro Nacional de Cultura.

25 For instance at the European summit conference at Madrid in December 1995.

26 Ole Waever, 'Europe's three empires. A Watsonian interpretation of postwar European security', in Rick Fawn and Jeremy Larkins (eds) *International Society After the Cold War; Anarchy and Order Reconsidered*, Macmillan, 1996, pp. 220–60.

3 Decolonization and its consequences

Of all the great tides of events that have shaped the affairs of human-kind in recent centuries, none has affected more people and had more lasting consequences than the flood of European expansion over the rest of the world. European imperial rule, the direct administration of territories outside Europe, has now almost entirely ebbed. But the effects of European domination are profound and seemingly lasting. The Americas and Australasia are now largely settled by peoples of European stock. In Asia and Africa the educated minorities that govern and administer both the public and private sectors have almost all adopted European forms and technology and even Euro-pean dress. In Asia the cultures are now a blend of their ancient civil-izations and the practices and values of the Europeans; in Africa and Oceania Europeanization has been even more radical.

Other empires too have left a similar enduring imprint. The spread of Islam through imperial expansion is one example. So is the Roman-ization of the lands between the Rhine and the strait of Gibraltar. The peoples of those areas cherish much of what they learnt from their former conquerors. If an imperial Roman could visit the French- and Portuguese-speaking states of Africa today, he would recognize that in all of them the language of governance and education is derived from his own, and used for much the same purposes as Latin was in Gaul and Lusitania. But former empires were regional: the European imprint is the first to be world-wide.

We are concerned here with one aspect of the European flood. Everywhere the Europeans went they established, sooner or later, dependent states on European lines. One of the most important changes in the nature of our international society in this century has been the dissolution of the empires and the achievement of independence by a long list of dependent and colonial territories. The numbers themselves are impressive: Over two thirds of the present members of the United Nations were once European (including Russian) dependencies, and more than half have achieved or regained independence since the Second World War. In this chapter, I want first to see what sort of states these were at the time of their independence, and what their ties were to the European imperial powers. Second, I want to examine the economic and strategic limits to their present independence, or in other words how much freedom of action their governments have in fact attained. Third I want to look at some consequences of the wholesale decolonization we have experienced. Decolonization meant cutting certain ties which bound the newly independent states to individual European powers. How has the severing of those bonds affected the pressures of increasing involvement of states with one another? What other ties have taken the place of the severed colonial ones? And how have so many strongly asserted new independences affected the rules and institutions, and the unwritten codes of conduct, of the international society which the Europeans worked out to manage their involvement, and then applied to the rest of the world? The conflict between these independences and Western standards of civilization and human rights are discussed in Chapter 5.

EUROPEAN EXPANSION

The empires that have dissolved in the twentieth century were, except for the Ottoman Turkish empire and the Japanese possessions, founded by peoples of European stock. Why did Europeans from the western margins of the continent sail out to establish a patchwork of maritime empires and involve the rest of the world with themselves? Why did Russians on the eastern margin of Europe expand by land into Asia, sometimes into highly civilized countries, but without a territorial break? The answers will help us to understand the relationship of the newly independent states to today's world economy and the world strategic pattern.

There were many reasons. New European techniques, especially in navigation, made maritime expansion possible. Religious motives, such as animated missionaries and the puritans in the Mayflower; a love of adventure; the desire for new land to settle; wars with other Europeans: all played their part. But from Columbus' attempt to reach the Indies and the Russian traders who first planted the double eagle flag on the Pacific, *the main driving force was economic*; colonization was carried out mainly by or on behalf of traders.

Columbus's aim to reach the Indies is a reminder that for millenia there had been a trickle, and sometimes more than a trickle, of trade between Europe and the high civilizations of Asia, along the silk road and across the Arabian Sea. In Africa Arab and later especially European traders created a demand for a wide range of goods from knives to cloth and salt; the question for Africans was how to pay for what the outsiders were willing to sell.

The traders and settlers involved their governments. They usually operated under various forms of government charter. The decisive action of the Europeans as they expanded was to establish **dependent states on the European model**, with European concepts and practices of statehood, linked to Europe. Some overseas colonies were founded by West European settlers, in areas with suitable climates and areas sparsely inhabited by pre-literate peoples. The settlers were not self-sufficient: they were extensions of Europe. They remained a part of European culture. They needed the mother country's military protection against other Europeans and sometimes against local peoples too. Above all they needed to import a whole range of goods from Europe; and they had to produce exports for the European market that would enable them to buy what they wanted. They shipped back to Europe gold and silver; sugar, tobacco and similar commodities; furs and fish. Russian expansion into the spaces left by the Tartars was gradual and cumulative, like the American moving frontier. The Russian settlers and traders who colonized new lands 'with the icon and the axe' were also dependent on the mother country, and saw themselves as extensions of it.

In lands that were not suitable for European settlement – Asia and tropical America, and later Africa – the significant overseas ventures of the West Europeans were more specifically economic. The competing merchant organizers were not primarily concerned with exports, as so many private companies are today. They wanted to purchase, or where necessary to produce, goods that could be shipped back to Europe, at high risk but if successful at great profit. Before the nineteenth century the high civilizations of Asia seemed to the Europeans in many ways more advanced than their own, and able to produce finer goods than they could make at home. Of course the fine manufactures and commodities like tea and spices had to be traded, *at prices set by the Asians*, for whatever the Asians would accept in exchange. The economic activities of the Dutch, British and French in the East were organized by East India Companies.[1] Those merchant companies, rather than the governments of the European states, felt that certain military and later also administrative responsibilities were necessary to safeguard their commercial enterprises. The merchants wanted to ensure the reliable production of the goods that they wanted to ship home. So the companies gradually acquired the capacity to establish local alliances and fend off rival Europeans, and more significantly to administer and **maintain order** in certain key territories and along trade routes, nominally on behalf of Asian rulers. For instance, the British East India Company administered the areas it controlled by delegation from and on behalf of the Mughal emperors. Until the nineteenth century the West European relationship with Asia beyond the Mediterranean was mercantile, radial and distant (two months or more away by sea in either direction). It was also one of competition and conflict, with few limits to independent action. It was a free-for-all of private enterprise, much of it beyond the control of European governments, who kept a looser rein on what happened overseas than in Europe itself.

Certain continuities in the economic patterns set up by European expansion are worth noting at this point. The present economic relationship between the West and an Asia that has regained control over its affairs is not so different from what it was before the nineteenth century. One difference is that the Asians are somewhat more eager to sell, and the West slightly less eager to buy. But for instance the problem of Japan's current trade imbalances – that is, of what Europe and North America can sell to Japan, in return for the large quantities of sophisticated Japanese goods that Westerners want – would be all too familiar to the East India Companies.

THE LEGACY OF THE DEPENDENT STATES

The nineteenth century saw a big change. The Europeans came to dominate the world; and world history, now unified into a single story for the first time, became Eurocentric. It has been aptly said that during that century Clio herself was a blonde.

European technology, with its new techniques in fields ranging from medicine to government, would have been diffused if there had been no European imperialism; but the process would have been much slower and less general. The Chinese, the Indians, the world of high Islam, also diffused the know-how of their advanced civilizations to less developed societies, but only gradually.

Four factors chiefly determined Europe's impact on other countries during its brief but fateful domination of the world. The first was technology, which gave the Europeans overwhelming economic and military superiority. The second was the establishment of a world order. The third was the creation of Western-educated elites. The fourth was the idea of independent sovereignty for all dependent states.

The industrial and technological revolution which we noted in Chapter 1 produced a quantum leap in the **economic and military power** of the Europeans, which gave them a century of dominance. In the age of imperialism, Europeans regarded dominions outside Europe over palm and pine as bringing glory and prestige as well as strategic and economic benefits. In that age the technical superiority which the industrial revolution gave to Europeans, and which made their imperialism possible, also stimulated an intoxicating sense of cultural, moral and racial superiority. With it went, in the minds of most Europeans, a flattering but genuine acceptance of a moral obligation to impart the benefits of Europe's superior civilization to others.

The second factor was **world order.** Two aspects of this problem confronted the imperial powers. Their solutions to both survive in modified form. The first was order in the dependent territories, the imposition by European states of an imperial pax. The establishment of the pax required military operations. The second was the maintenance of order between European powers and their nationals outside Europe, and between them and independent non-European states.

The Concert of Europe brought much needed **order** to European expansion, across the seas and in Russia's case by land. The conflicts of the merchants and settlers came to an end. In place of intermittent and uncontrolled violence the imperial powers were able to agree on an extending partition of the eastern hemisphere, which tacitly accepted the dominance of each individual government in specific areas.

The attitude of the imperial governments, which almost amounted to a sense of common or parallel enterprise, is well conveyed in a circular despatch sent by the statesmanlike Russian Foreign Minister, Prince Gorchakov, to the Tsar's ambassadors in other imperial capitals. In 1864, a few years after the Crimean War blocked the Russian advance into the Ottoman empire, the Russians resumed their expansion further east in Central Asia. 'In case questions are asked, or you see erroneous ideas, about our action in those distant parts,' Gorchakov instructed his ambassadors, they should use the following formula as a guide.

> The position of Russia in Central Asia is that of all civilized states which are brought into contact with half-savage nomad populations possessing no fixed social organization.
>
> In such cases it always happens that the more civilized state is forced, in the interests of the security of its frontier and its commercial relations, to exercise a certain ascendancy over those whom

their turbulent and unsettled character make most undesirable neighbours.

The dilemma of any civilized state, Gorchakov wrote, was that if it is not to give up trying to civilize and protect the areas already under its authority, it will find itself drawn 'deeper and deeper into barbarous areas'. In a striking passage he put Russia's policy, and the need for restraint, in a general context.

> Such has been the fate of every country which has found itself in a similar position. The United States in America, France in Algeria, Holland in her colonies, England in India – all have been irresistibly forced, less by ambition than by imperious necessity, into this onward movement where the greatest difficulty is to know where to stop.

'It is urgent' Gorchakov went on, 'to escape the danger of being carried away, as is almost inevitable, into an unlimited extension of territory.'[2]

Of course this despatch was intended as a justification of Russian expansion. But we should not miss Gorchakov's awareness of the force which his argument would have in London and Paris. In fact major powers (Gorchakov's first example was the United States) were being drawn into expansion outside Europe less by ambition than by necessity; and they recognized a moral obligation to carry out a civilizing mission. It was also in the spirit of the Concert of Europe for a great power to let its concert partners know in advance what it intended to do. Indeed the British Foreign Secretary suggested that the two powers should formally agree that when either felt compelled to expand in Asia, it would tell the other its reasons and the extent of the contemplated increase of territory; but Gorchakov preferred to leave the obligation voluntary.

The agreed expansion of European authority reached a second climax in the partition of the interior of Africa at Berlin in the 1880s. The colonization of the interior of tropical Africa covered a remarkably short span of time. Administration of the new dependent states was not effectively in place until about 1900; in much of Africa the reins were handed over to Africans in the early 1960s. Travelling around Africa at the time of independence I met many people in different states who remembered the arrival of the white administrators and had lived to see them go. In that brief period of sixty years the colonizing powers put into place the state structures that have now been taken over by Africans.

When Europeans assumed administrative responsibilities in territories unsuitable for European settlement, they found a wide variety of governmental structures, ranging from the sophisticated urban polities of India and Java to what Gorchakov called half-savage nomads and the pre-literate societies of Africa and the Pacific islands. The European administrators gradually transformed these structures into dependent states on the European model: similar to those established by the European settlers, but more directly controlled from Europe. Where the existing machinery of government seemed to them inadequate, they supplemented it with European administrative, judicial, police, defence, educational, medical and other functions, and in due course, legislatures. In Asia, especially India, several forms of indirect rule left local rulers and governments largely intact, and the changes were often minor. In Africa the European innovations were much more radical, and the administrators considered that their experiments with indirect rule were failures.[3]

The colonial and semi-colonial economies remained in the hands of private commercial enterprise, and were modified by European economic demand. In some cases, notably the Caribbean and South East Asia, but also parts of India and tropical Africa, the new dependent states fostered the growth of a plantation economy, which favoured the production of commodities like tea, coffee, rubber and sugar for developed markets.[4]

The establishment of order outside Europe did not merely require the statesmen of the imperial powers to agree on, or acquiesce in, their parallel expansions. They also had to manage the day-to-day contacts and potential frictions which their agreed expansion produced on the ground. What arrangements should regulate the new extended states system? The obvious way to deal with non-European countries which were not directly administered by a European power, was to adapt to the varying local circumstances the transcultural capitulations which regulated European dealings with the Ottoman empire. The imperial powers consequently set up various arrangements of the same kind from Morocco to China. But between themselves the European states had developed rules and institutions of order and restraint within the cultural matrix of their *grande république*. After the Napoleonic wars the Europeans increasingly applied these rules and institutions to their dealings with each other outside Europe, and to their dealings with non-European states.

In this way the Europeans were also able to manage the pressures and interests of a states system that had expanded to cover the whole world. In other words the power of the industrial revolution and the management of international affairs by the European concert, taken together, made the world much more orderly than what had prevailed before, and set much firmer limits to the independent actions of states and also of private operators. It is surely remarkable that in the whole century between the fall of Napoleon and the start of the First World War, there were no military conflicts between European powers outside Europe except the Crimean War, and that was largely about the position of Turkey in Europe.

Both European superior economic and military power and the establishment of a worldwide European order tended to push the new international system, and the conscious management of it, along the spectrum away from its previous disorder towards tighter restraints and greater hegemonial authority. On the other hand the third and fourth features of the expansion of Europe mentioned above began to pull the new international society more slowly and less conspicuously the opposite way, towards more absolute and more multiple independences, with less limits on freedom of action.

The third factor was the desire of non-Europeans to 'learn how the white man does it'. The high civilizations of Asia like India, China and Japan had previously had a technical as well as (in their own eyes and in the eyes of some Europeans) cultural superiority. In the nineteenth century increasing numbers of Asians came to realize that in practical matters, such as manufacturing techniques and the arts of war and peace, including the art of government, they now had much to learn from the Europeans. Moreover the manifestly superior power and competence of the Europeans seemed to non-Europeans to be more absolute and permanent than it has since turned out to be. In less developed pre-literate areas like tropical Africa and the Pacific, the difference between European and local levels of civilization was much more marked than in Asia. People had to learn, not just to read and write French or English, but what reading and writing were.[5]

Most of the European education of non-Europeans was acquired on the spot. But as the century progressed, Oxford, Cambridge and the London School of Economics, the Sorbonne, the Universities of Lisbon and Coimbra and the Dutch universities, and also significantly the military colleges, accepted increasing numbers of Asian and African students. The numbers grew in the first half of this century, augmented by the corresponding facilities in the United States, and the stream continues today. **Western-educated elites** came into being, who were familiar both with their own culture and with that of the imperial power. Major figures like Nehru, Ho Chi-Minh, Senghor, Benazir Bhutto and the King of Jordan are conspicuous names in a long list. Asians in the Russian empire learnt Russian and tsarist or Stalinist ways, and added Russian endings to their islamic names.

In imperial systems these elites acted to some extent as intermediaries between the two cultures, and were therefore particularly useful to the imperial authorities. The issue is discussed at greater length in the next chapter. The cultural and technical familiarity of the non-Western elites with Western thought and know-how played and still plays a vital role in their understanding of modern states, government and the rules and practices of international society. But the familiarity of the elites with the West did not usually engender in them any loyalty to the imperial power. One of the values they learnt from the Europeans was the case for their own sovereign independence.

The fourth factor, then, was the desire of the non-Europeans to achieve **independent sovereignty.** We saw that it animated every dependent prince and ruler in Europe, and also led powerful groups among the European settlers to demand independence. When British and Spanish settler dependencies in the Americas became independent, the new governments insisted on very full freedom of action, and avoided becoming entangled in the alliances and other constraints set by the European society of states.

In Asia and elsewhere Western-educated local elites soon occupied administrative positions in the governments of the non-settler European dependencies. In due course the elites both in and outside government voiced the opinion, derived from the Americas and from Europe, that the states set up by the imperial powers should be turned over entirely to them, in the same way as the American states had been turned over to the settlers. They wanted to cut the ties to the imperial power, but to preserve the administrative structure and frontiers of their state. Internally they did not want to destroy the European machinery of government: they wanted to take it over. Externally they did not want to secede from the worldwide international society that the Europeans had created: they wanted to join it as full juridical equals. And like the American settlers they wanted to avoid entangling alliances, to be non-aligned. The pattern of twentieth-century decolonization was beginning to take shape.

DECOLONIZATION: EUROPEAN ATTITUDES

The decisive first step of decolonization was the massive achievement of political independence by many settler colonies in the Americas (circa 1770–1830). So long as the French imperial design threatened the British settlers, they needed and welcomed British imperial protection. But when the French threat collapsed, the colonists could afford independence and even felt able to accept French help in achieving it. They wanted independence, both strategic and economic, in order to develop their ideas of democracy and to conduct their commerce to their best advantage. The Spanish American settlers also wanted to control their commerce with Europe, though they preferred government which was more authoritarian than the North American form of democracy. But in both cases independence was associated with democracy in its broad sense, or at least with implementing the will of a majority of the settlers.

The secessions of American colonies fostered among Europeans an acquiescence in independence for other overseas dependencies, and in some cases an active encouragement.[6] Burke, the Member of Parliament for Bristol, a port that lived by the America trade, was one of the first to perceive that if a group of colonists wanted to secede, the imperial power would be better off on balance if it let them go. In early nineteenth-century Europe many held that when a colony became ripe it would drop from the tree, and they noted that in classical Greece, that model for the Victorian age, settler colonies were independent from the start. By the beginning of the twentieth century, dependencies where European settlers formed a majority of the population – Canada, Brazil, Australia, New Zealand – had acquired as much independence as they wanted.

The road to independence, either by rebellion or negotiation, had been clear for settlers. But this was not the case for non-settler, administrative colonies. The second half of the nineteenth century was the age of European state imperialism in the eastern hemisphere. Governments took over the administrative responsibilities that had become too much for private companies. One consequence of the expansion of the authority of European democratic states was that missionary, abolitionist and liberal opinion in Europe became increasingly concerned with the welfare of the non-Europeans who were being brought under European authority and for whom European governments had a responsibility. The commitment to the welfare of the governed was formulated in a number of government declarations, which were often disregarded but gradually altered the conduct of European authorities in Asia and Africa. Thus a British parliamentary committee on India of 1833 proclaimed in strong language 'the indisputable-principle that the interests of the native subjects are to be consulted in preference to those of Europeans whenever the two come in competition'. The Berlin agreement on Africa gave the principle international endorsement by declaring that the welfare of the native populations must be paramount.

The Europeans (including Russians and North Americans) took it for granted that the responsibility would best be discharged by imparting to non-Europeans the benefits of the progress achieved in Europe. Black Africans and some other peoples with pre-literate cultures were still regarded as savages – noble savages, perhaps, but in need of civilization. Even the high civilizations of Asia, for which there was considerable respect, were to be brought up to the **standards of civilization** which had been developed in Europe and North America, and which the imperial powers assumed to be of universal validity. The task was not easy: the white man's burden really was a burden to the missionaries and administrators, the doctors and teachers, in non-Western countries. The Europeans who benefited most from colonial rule were businessmen and traders.

The responsibilities towards the local populations proclaimed at Berlin continued to be partially applied. In the early part of the twentieth century the League of Nations mandates made the primacy of local welfare and eventual decolonization more explicit. The League mandates applied only to former German and Ottoman territories, but the principles that underlay the mandate provisions inevitably affected policy in other colonies as well. After the Second World War the mandate principles were reaffirmed in the United Nations trusteeships. The international agreements drawn up by the Western powers specifically legitimized (in their eyes) the inequality of states and cultural entities, and listed some of them specifically according to their degree of readiness for self-government. The mandates and trusteeships continued to entrust to European states and settler states of European descent the job of bringing less-developed peoples to the standards required for independence.[7]

In other words, the League and the UN recognized a category of dependent states, and the obligation of donors to aid them to achieve the standards of civilization necessary for sovereign statehood. The UN General Assembly reversed this position in 1960 by declaring that 'the inadequacy of political, economic, social or educational preparedness should never serve as a pretext for delaying independence'. That anarchophile spirit did not last. It is now acceptable again to think openly about unequal relations between states, and to act accordingly, so long as nominal independence is acknowledged. The obligations of donor states and the dependence in practice of recipients today are discussed further in Chapters 4 and 7.

In the eyes of the imperial powers the settlers were Europeans, white people, and could be assumed to have adequate standards of civilization. Non-European peoples, or at least governing circles, must achieve European standards in order to be accepted as independent members of international society. Western standards became more demanding: they began to include not merely commercial law and safety for Europeans and their property, but also such concepts as democracy and the position of women. But conversely it was understood that once standards of (Western) civilization were attained, non-European peoples should become full citizens either of independent states or of an expanded imperial state. The Europeans were beginning to foresee the end of their empires, and to think about post-imperial arrangements. The attitudes of Europeans and North Americans a century ago about inducing others to observe civilized standards may seem very different from the way Westerners think today. But the same attitudes in fact continue actively in modified and non-racial forms. We will look at the issue in more detail in Chapter 5.

Between the two world wars the belief in the advantages of empire continued to be general in the colonizing powers, which included the United States, and it lingered in many people's minds after World War II. The nationalist publics of the European imperial powers were slow to realize that colonies might look nice on a map but that by the middle of the twentieth century they had come to cost more money and blood than they were worth. Yet in the inter-war period governments and administrators were beginning to feel that decolonization within the imperial conglomerates was acceptable. Variants of this solution began to be implemented. The French held elections in some colonies to the imperial parliament in Paris; the British granted independence to Iraq. I was taught in school in the early 1930s that India would achieve full self-government in the 1940s 'like Canada and Australia', which indeed it did. These ideas, and the weakness of European governments, led to the effective decolonization of almost all Asian dependent states outside the Soviet Union shortly after the Second World War.

After that war, and nearly two centuries after Burke, the disadvantages to an imperial power of resisting by force an armed rebellion in favour of independence became clear to most Europeans. Multiple independences became intellectually fashionable. Ideas of racial superiority seemed increasingly shameful. By 1960 governments and public opinion in democratic Britain, France and Belgium, and public opinion increasingly in Salazar Portugal and Franco Spain, were disillusioned about colonialism. They considered it unwise, and perhaps also morally wrong, to refuse any significant demand for independence by a Westernized elite. A widely read Portuguese book, *A Gadanha da Mort* (The Scythe of Death) asked the memorable question: 'What are our sons fighting for in Africa? So that their sons can in due course also fight in Africa?' The sense that it was better to let go was increased by the pressure of both superpowers on the Europeans to grant immediate independence, though the superpowers themselves were not so ready to decolonize.

The proliferation of weak and inexperienced states, and the handing over of great areas of the globe to them, clearly involved a loosening of the structure of international society. In the post-imperial age that did not seem a forbidding objection, and certainly not as destabilizing as armed conflict between colonial insurgents and imperial powers. Where such conflicts took place on a large scale, as in Vietnam and in Angola and Mozambique, the insurgents and independence-minded elites turned to communists for organization and ideology, which made the military option even less attractive to the West.

So it was that soon after the Suez débacle of 1956 most of the remaining west European dependencies obtained their independence by amicable agreement. Most dependencies in Asia were already independent, and apparently managing very adequately. For the imperial governments of Western Europe, decolonization had become a matter of calculated self-interest. Inside those governments, and in diplomatic discussions between them (in many of which I took part) the arguments of expediency prevailed. Moral obligation was put forward rather by those who thought that imperial authority ought to remain in parts of Africa, the Caribbean and Oceania until it had brought the local population to levels of democracy and administrative competence adequate to run a modern state on European lines – in other words by those who still accepted the obligation underlying the League mandates and the UN trusteeships. But left-wing and especially Marxist circles in Europe, and almost the whole of public opinion in the United States, considered colonialism morally wrong and something to be abolished like slavery.

In the eyes of the Europeans and European settlers, decolonization could be achieved in two ways: either non-Europeans could learn how to govern a modern state by serving an apprenticeship in a colonial or dependent state, in which power would be transferred to them in stages, or else non-European populations, especially pre-literate ones, could be 'romanized'; that is, assimilated into the civilization of the

imperial power, and progressively given a say in the imperial government, for instance by voting rights in empire-wide elections.

The first course was preferred by the British. They kept the government of the United Kingdom to themselves, and progressively meted
out doses of self-government to the point of full political independence. They applied this devolutionary procedure first to the settler
states or white dominions and then to all the dependent states of
their imperial conglomerate that were willing to accept it. Most of
these states on achieving independence chose to remain associated in
a loose and voluntary Commonwealth, that has survived in an attenuated form to the present day and provides certain benefits to its less
developed members.

The French and Portuguese tried the path of romanization, which
reflected their own history. In the early phases of decolonization
French governments declared that France was a nation of a hundred
million, extended citizenship and the franchise, and accepted adequately assimilated non-Europeans into their legislature. The most
eminent, like Léopold Senghor, later President of Senegal, and Félix
Houphouet-Boigny, later President of the Ivory Coast, became cabinet
ministers. The Portuguese had a similar, but under Salazar slower,
policy of romanization. The romanization policy was not politically
successful. The French and Portuguese African colonies, led by their
Westernized elites, all opted for separate statehood. Only a few
small territories, mainly islands with a settler presence like Martinique
and Tahiti, have become overseas departments of France.

There has been much discussion about the element of racism in the
decolonization policies of the imperial powers. In the imperial period
feelings of racial superiority were common amongst Europeans, and
were often manifested in what seems to us an ugly way. Race prejudice
was rarest amongst the Portuguese: governments in Lisbon dis-
couraged it and for some time subsidized interracial marriages.
Romanization is manifestly non-racist, since it involves deliberately
incorporating individuals from other races as citizens. The Roman
Emperor Caracalla's decision to extend Roman citizenship to all free
men in the empire was not racist. On the other hand romanization
does reflect an attitude of cultural superiority. Whether or not assimilated individuals retain a religion such as Islam and some elements of
their own culture, romanization requires them to accept a European
culture and values. The French and Portuguese policies of romanization have had a considerable cultural success. The elites of franco-
phone and lusophone Africa are more deeply attuned to European
culture than their equivalents in English-speaking Africa. The British

policy of not incorporating the British West Indies, for instance, into the United Kingdom but insisting on separate statehoods for them, can be described as exclusivist; but separate independences for the islands can be called discriminatory only if incorporation as a minority element in a rich and developed European state is considered to be preferable on balance to independence in a micro-state of one's own. This issue is discussed further in the next chapter.

The decolonization policies of the two superpowers, the United States and Russia, fit into this general pattern. The United States has never admitted that its overseas dependencies were colonies, but that is a question of labels not substance.[8] It has given independence to some, such as the Philippines; granted federal statehood on an equal footing to others like Hawaii; and continues to administer other islands in the Caribbean and the Pacific as partially self-governing dependencies.

In Russia Lenin and then Stalin professed to decolonize the tsarist empire by including the Russian dependencies in the Union of Soviet Republics on an equal footing with the Russians. It was a symbolic decolonization, but under a totalitarian dictatorship it made little difference in practice. Under Stalin's policy, contemptuously but aptly described by the American diplomat Charles Bohlen as 'folk songs and the firing squad', Russian cultural assimilation continued. But political ideas from abroad filtered into the non-Russian states of the Soviet Union. The formula of self-determination, the idealization of the nation–state and the re-awakening of Islam fostered the desire to dissolve the Russian empire into multiple independences in the same way as the other European empires whose demise had been gleefully reported by official Soviet propaganda.[9]

Russian imperial authority in central Asia, from Gorchakov to Gorbachev, lasted a century and a quarter. That is appreciably longer than West European rule in the interior of Africa, but a decade or two less than effective British dominion over India. All are short periods by historical standards. The collapse of the Soviet Union brought quick and absolute nominal independences. The new governments of the non-European empire have, like other recently decolonized dependencies, retained the administrative boundaries set by the Soviets and are composed of Russian-educated elites. As was also to be expected, most are now markedly more authoritarian than Russia itself. What the limits to the independence of the Asian and Caucasian states will amount to in practice, and what will remain of their relationship to Russia, is still very uncertain. They are already looking outside their borders for help.

ATTITUDES IN THE DEPENDENCIES

The European-educated elites of states which recovered their independence, or acquired it for the first time, since the Second World War have insisted on decolonization to full political sovereignty. By 1960 it seemed to the international society as a whole, and not least to the decolonizing imperial powers, that faced with these demands the right or at least the prudent course was to grant sovereign statehood and UN membership to more or less every dependent territory that wanted it. Even very small states or islands whose inhabitants measured by objective criteria hardly yet had a capacity for self-government or for playing a meaningful minor role in international affairs – who in the jargon of the time hardly constituted a nation – achieved political independence. No other formula or intermediate autonomy was available to offer them.

Decolonization gave the United Nations, with its associated institutions like the World Bank, new functions. Membership has become the determining legitimation of independent status. The UN provides a universal forum where smaller states can make their voices heard. It provides collective machinery for many kinds of aid. And the end of the cold war has enabled the Security Council to legitimize action by the great powers where they agree. These are valuable secondary tasks. In the era of decolonization the UN was an essential institution of the international society of proliferating independences.

The formal legitimacy of independence is a status: a category in diplomacy, at the United Nations and in international law. But it does not describe absolute control of foreign and domestic policy. The interests and pressures of the states system continue to operate. The rules of the international society, and most pertinently the conditions of the assistance which weak states need, are determined by the great and rich powers and the organizations which they substantially control, especially the economic ones. Newly independent states find themselves much constrained by the pressures of the system, the rules of the society and the hegemonial say-so of the great powers.

The problem of administrative or political decolonization – what is popularly called the **transfer of power** – was how local Western-educated elites could take over governing authority with the minimum of disruption. It was predictable and expected that the higher the level of government achieved before the Europeans established dependent states, the smoother and less disruptive the transfer of administration back out of European hands would be. The highest levels of pre-colonial achievement were in Asia. Decolonization there led to effective government, even in the minority of cases where those who took over power had resorted to force against the imperial government. In the great majority of cases, in Asia and also where the level of competence was much lower, the administration of European dependencies was handed over by mutual agreement, after negotiations which were chiefly concerned with what assistance the former imperial power would continue to provide after independence.

The Western-trained elites who stepped into the shoes of the imperial authority had a more authoritarian outlook on governance than liberal and socialist public opinion in the West. They thought in terms of a strong executive power like that exercised by the imperial governors. They understood more clearly than their European and American supporters that colonial administration had been introduced into their territories primarily to maintain order; that their recently created states were fragile; and that disorder and the disruption of the economy were real and serious threats to their ability to govern. They therefore realized the need to 'govern firmly'. But some of them are not able to govern firmly enough. The authority of several of the states set up by the Europeans is diminishing fast; and the turbulence in much of black Africa could become so unmanageable that the structure, the degree of autonomy and even the boundaries of existing states may radically change. The conflict between decolonized firm government and current Western standards of democracy and human rights is discussed in Chapter 5.

The views of the Western-educated elites on decolonization were loudly expounded and echoed. What did the men and women in the streets of the European-built cities of other continents, on the land, and in the still-tribal African bush think and feel? In Asia there seems to have been a general feeling of relief, a sense of resuming a modified version of their former ways of government. Elsewhere the impact of European colonization was greater. I was in several African countries at or close to the moment of their formal independence. There and later round the Caribbean I tried to find, or at least collect, answers to this question. These I have added to what others have been able to tell me.

It seemed to me that by and large, the mass of the people in colonial territories were pleased by independence. Many of them had been organized into mass parties by the elites, and accepted the aims of those parties. The colonial administrators were very alien, and most people much prefer to be governed by their own kind. There was little or no expectation of a reversion to pre-colonial times. Many less-educated people expected the new administrators to govern in much the same way as the British district commissioners, French *commandants de cercle* or Portuguese *administradores* that they were used to, perhaps with rather more acceptance of local ways. In Africa the simpler people still had strong tribal allegiances, which covered not only clan loyalty but also attachment to a distinctive way of life, from the semi-nomadic Fulas or Peulhs, Masai and Somalis to matriarchal fisher people like the Bissagos islanders. Such people had only a hazy concept of a modern European-style state, and did not feel themselves to be its citizens in a Western sense.

The **economic problems** were different. The civilizations of East and South Asia were economically and administratively highly developed in the early centuries of contact, and their millenial skills provided the economic incentive to European traders. Not surprisingly, the states established by the Europeans or modelled after them in those areas have found it fairly easy to advance beyond a plantation and simple industrial economy dominated by the colonizers, and to resume the production and export of the most sophisticated goods available. There were of course people like Gandhi who saw and feared the dangers of economic development, just as people like Tolstoy and the Amish did in Europe and the Americas. But the material advantages of development had the stronger pull. The economies of almost all the Asian states are growing faster than those of Europe, and have now regained or are moving rapidly towards the economic parity with the West that they had before the industrial revolution gave the Europeans a great but temporary advantage. The Asian states have broadened their dealings with the rest of the world, and diminished the relative importance of the former imperial power to their economies. In short, most Asian states have emerged or are emerging from 'third-world status' and are taking their places as economic partners of the developed world on a genuinely equal footing.

In Africa, Oceania and the Caribbean the new states are unable to produce or pay for the whole huge range of goods and services, from consumer, medical and other products to technical and administrative know-how, that are more necessary today than at any previous time. The rising expectations of an increasing population have a double multiplying effect on demand. Almost all the governments of such countries are therefore eager to receive whatever they can in the form of loans, grants, and technical assistance. They also increasingly feel the need to export, both in order to buy the goods and services they or their peoples want, and to establish an adequate credit rating by paying at least the interest on their loans. The governments accordingly encourage the production of goods, and of services such as tourism, that the rest of the world is willing to buy.

In short, the new governments face the problems of supplying, and of creating conditions in which it is possible to produce whatever helps to meet their peoples' insistent and rising demand. The problem of how to create such conditions has been the nub of the relation of these areas to the developed West since substantial contacts first developed. It is not surprising that the relationship of tropical Africa and the Caribbean to the developed areas of the world is basically still what it was a century ago.

But there is an essential difference. In the colonial era the imperial powers in effect divided up the dependent areas of the world, by tacit consent or formal agreement, into areas of single-power responsibility. There were areas of joint responsibility for order, commerce and standards of civilization, like China and Morocco; but these were exceptions. Consequently the economies of the dependent states were focussed on that of the imperial power, for that was where the decisions on economic development were taken, both by the imperial government and by imperial commercial enterprises. The new governments can within limits take their own decisions. They do not want to depend more than necessary on the former imperial power. They want to spread their dependence as widely as possible, with as few conditions as possible. They prefer aid from multilateral international agencies to aid whose conditions are set by any single power. Even so, it is still dependence.

The developed states for their part have been willing to assume collectively a modified form of the role which the imperial powers played individually in the colonial phase. The need of the dependent governments for collective economic security is so acute that the industrialized countries are not only able to set the terms for trade and for the wide range of forms which aid now takes. They are also, and increasingly since the collapse of the Soviet Union, able to influence the internal governance of most of the newly independent states. This puts rich Western powers in a position to demand as the price of their aid that the recipient states should observe, at least to some extent, the standards of civilization now current in the West. In some ways the relation of the developed world to the states of Africa and the Caribbean is like the former relation of the West to China: 'the world community' recognizes their nominal independence, but may apply pressure or intervene in a state that is unable to govern itself according to Western standards. Some consequences of this new relationship will be examined in the next chapters.

DECOLONIZATION IN PERSPECTIVE

I do not want to pass a judgement on the long story of decolonization, or on its last phases since the Second World War. Indeed, what standards or criteria one would use in arriving at a verdict, I do not know. But perhaps we can begin to see it as something that has now taken place, and to assess what it was and what its consequences are.

We started our enquiry in Chapter 1 with technology; and that is the key to understanding the global expansion of the Europeans. At first the Westerners had an edge only in navigation and gunnery: European superiority in Asia did not become significant until the nineteenth century. Those on the margins of Europe (Iberians, British, Russians) were impelled, one might almost say sucked, into the rest of the world by the relative superiority of their know-how, and by the profitable long-distance trade which their know-how made possible. The conscious motives of the Europeans were mixed. The most important was trade, conducted by merchants. The settler colonies, mainly extensions of the fringes of Europe, needed to buy so much from Europe that they too were very much concerned with trade. Some implications of the key role played by economic enterprise in the integration of the world are discussed in Chapter 7.

The nineteenth-century colonial empires, almost entirely in the eastern hemisphere, were more imperial. Their purpose was to establish the security, technology and order that would facilitate the production and exchange of goods. This purpose they achieved. A further result of European state imperialism was to increase the interdependence of different parts of the world, and to extend the economic unification explored by private commercial enterprises into an integrated global states system and a worldwide international society, under European control and with European rules and standards.

When the tide of European expansion ebbed, as it was bound to do, much of what it had brought to the rest of the world remained. The independence of the settler colonies in the Americas and Australasia pointed the way for the recent general decolonization of the largely non-European dependencies elsewhere. Decolonization did not aim to undo the essential achievements of European expansion. The issue for both the settlers and the European-educated elites was: what new arrangements would continue the desirable achievements of colonialism while getting rid of the undesirable ones? The Westernized rulers of the recently independent states wanted to end European rule and the enforcement of European standards, but to preserve and take over the states created by the Europeans. The new governments also wanted to remain in the global international society, which gave them status as equal members, protected them against aggression, and helped to pay for what the poorer states needed; though they wanted the society of states to be a good deal looser – more anarchical in the technical sense – than it had been under colonialism. More prosaically they also needed to maintain and improve their economic relations with developed countries: a need which was very real indeed.

The following formula may help put decolonization in its historical context. The establishment of imperial authority, even a number of competing imperial authorities, obviously tightens a system of interacting states, and moves it further towards the centralized end of the spectrum; and decolonization has the opposite effect. The decolonization of most of the mainland of the Americas (circa 1770–1830) was a significant loosening of political and strategic (but not economic) integration across the Atlantic, a move towards multiple and effective independences. In the nineteenth century the pendulum swung back to a tighter system. The whole eastern hemisphere was politically and strategically integrated under European dominance. But the relative supremacy of the West did not last. Japan and some other East Asian states have now caught up with western technology. The most lasting result of European dominance is the economic integration of the planet.

The great decolonization since World War II was designed to reverse once more the trend towards imperial political integration. Its rhetoric demanded a general fragmentation and non-alignment. Taken together with the polarization of the cold war, the liquidation of the Western colonial empires seemed to some people to threaten the virtual disintegration of a large part of the international system. Such fears were exaggerated. In fact the newly independent states, almost without exception, soon showed that they were anxious not to revert to the position before European expansion. The world remained economically (and also strategically) integrated. The difference was that the responsibility for security and order had been transferred to the Western-educated elites.

European (including US and Russian) domination and administrative control of non-European areas was like an overlay, which decolonization removed. But the non-European areas did not and could not revert to what was there before. When the man in the iron mask had his mask removed, his face had assumed the features of the mask. There have been major changes, especially the economic reassertion of the East and South Asian half of mankind. But the states of Asia, Africa and Oceania are modelled structurally on European lines; the rules, institutions and many of the values of the society of states are essentially European; and the differing functions of most of the European-style states in the European-style society are still largely what they were before the imperial overlay was lifted.

After nearly half a century we can see that the achievements of the Asian states which acquired or resumed their independence before the collapse of the Soviet Union are the success story of the recent decolonization. On the other hand about half of the two hundred nominally independent members of today's international society cannot manage on their own and need a good deal of help.

The great powers for their part have been used since the Concert of Europe to think in terms of collective responsibility for order, and also for standards of civilization. At the low point of international society after the First World War some important major powers did not accept collective responsibilities. But in response to the continued dependence following decolonization, the developed countries have been willing, by and large, to accept collective responsibility for providing not only strategic but also economic security, and furthermore for ensuring some standards of what they consider civilized conduct, in about half the states members of the world community. The perception by the developed world that it is prudent as well as morally responsible to take on these unprecedented new commitments is *raison de système* on a global scale.

Consequently the crux of the relations of most newly independent states with the great, rich hegemonial powers is not just the external function of the new states in international society, though aid negotiations can be described in those terms. The issue centres very often on how the new governments run their internal affairs. The Western powers see themselves as having increased responsibilities towards the peoples of the new states, not just to their governments. In discharging these responsibilities they now increasingly often, collectively through international organizations and agreements or individually through the leverage of direct aid, overstep the theoretical line that bars foreigners from interference with the domestic governance of states. They do so on a wide range of issues from internal order and fiscal prudence to human rights. Overstepping that line was, in one sense, the essential feature of colonialism. The pendulum, after swinging far towards a host of new independences and the anarchic end of the spectrum, is now swinging back towards limits and restraints on the new states. The restraints are both economic and political. But they are mainly pragmatic rather than theoretical, and they leave intact the key legitimacy of nominal independence.

NOTES

1 The British East India Company 1600–1858, when the Government took over the direct administration of British India. The Dutch East India Company 1602–1788, after which the Government assumed the company's administrative responsibilities in what is now Indonesia. The French East India Company 1664–1769, dissolved after military defeats in India.

2 Text in Correspondence from 1864 to 1881 respecting the movements of Russia in Central Asia, Foreign Office 65\1202. For a background account see David Gillard's study of British and Russian imperialism, *The Struggle for Asia 1828–1914*, Methuen 1977, pp. 117–125.

3 One conspicuous exception was Lugard's policy of indirect rule in the Muslim emirates of Northern Nigeria. A good account based on first-hand experience is Margery Perham's *Lugard*, Collins 1960.

4 This study of the limits of independence is not the place to discuss the much-debated question of exploitation in colonial regimes. The debate tends to focus on plantation economies, and particularly on slave and indentured labour. At that stage there certainly was exploitation, greater than the corresponding 'wage slavery' in Europe. But in the earlier phase, the benefits which European traders derived from the great differences in price of Asian products in Asia and Europe can hardly be called exploitation. This is the fallacy exposed in the schoolboy economic example of the two islands, on one of which two oranges cost a banana while on the other two bananas cost an orange: trade was not exploitation. And the more Asian goods the Europeans, like the Arab middlemen before them, supplied to Europe, the more the price differentials shrank.

5 The Roman Empire offers an interesting parallel. The Hellenistic world had long been highly civilized, but the Romans had demonstrated a (temporary) superiority in war and government. Educated people in the Hellenistic East wanted to learn how their new Roman masters did it. Part of the interest of Polybius for students of modern imperialism is that his work is an explanation to his civilized Hellenistic fellows of the secrets of Roman success. But when the Romans turned their attention to my pre-literate ancestors in Britain, for instance, they had to begin almost from scratch.

6 British colonies in America seceded with French help, and Spanish colonies with British protection.

7 It is interesting to note that the Japanese government was proclaimed to be capable of assuming these responsibilities after World War I, while the Weimar government of Germany was not; but after World War II the Japanese and Italian governments were also declared unfit to act as trustees. But of course the self-interested decisions of the victors do not affect the concept that the international community could entrust to the most advanced of the victor states the responsibility for making less-advanced communities fit for self-government.

8 The point was illustrated for me by an eminent American lady in Washington in the 1950s. When she challenged me to name an American colony, I suggested Guam. To which she replied, 'Guam's not a colony. We *own* Guam!'

9 On this point see George Kennan's valuable article 'The End of the Empire' in the *New York Review of Books*, 16 November 1995.

4 Size, nationalism and imperial systems

DIFFERENCES BETWEEN STATES

States are not all alike. The international legitimacy of the day and the rules and institutions of our international society postulate that juridically they are all equal. We say that they are all members of international society and of bodies like the United Nations, which implies that they are much more like each other than they really are. Inis Claude calls the tendency to think of all states as if they were roughly the same kind of entity 'the myth of peas in the pod'.[1] 'The assertion that states are equal suggests that they are very much the same', he says. In fact they differ in size, far more than any dwarf differs from any giant: in our present system the largest have some 10,000 times the population of the smallest. They also differ in internal structure: forms of government, levels of economic and social development. And they function differently in the system. To say that juridically states are equal does not alter the reality of these differences. The concept that states are sufficiently alike to be treated as members of the same set is more than a fallacy. It is a myth which influences our concept of international reality and distorts our judgement.

It is sometimes said that of course we do not really think of the two hundred or so states in our system as alike, or even equal; but if we say they are, and conduct our international relations as if they were, perhaps they will become more so. This makes matters worse. We run afoul of Aristotle's dictum that injustice occurs when we treat unequals as equal. We make unreasonable demands on new and small political entities that have neither the size, nor the resources, nor the experience to respond. We also make it harder to manage the immense diversity of the political governance of the world in a discerning and constructive way.

The dependent states created by Europeans which achieved or regained their independence in the decolonization after the Second World War were of many kinds, and faced very different problems. For instance India, even without Pakistan, Bangladesh and Burma, inherited from the British and Mughal rajes immense problems of size and diversity, which it has so far managed encouragingly well. At the other end of the scale a number of mini-states are too small and too inexperienced to discharge adequately the responsibilities of statehood, or to focus the loyalties of their more educated inhabitants who are not directly involved in the new independent governments. This is not a new problem. In the fragmentary princedoms of Germany and Italy before unification, and in the Caribbean, inadequacy of size has presented difficulties that grow greater with increased independence.

The problems of inadequate size, experience and competence in newly independent states were borne in on me during my years as head of the African side of the Foreign Office (1956–59), my years as a roving British Ambassador in West Africa accredited to many new states as they became independent during the high tide of decolonization (1959–62) and my years in the Caribbean as British Ambassador to Cuba (1963–66).

PROBLEMS OF SIZE AND ADEQUACY

In most independent countries there is a growing awareness that political self-government and international recognition as a sovereign state is not the last stage on the road to complete independence, though it may be a decisive one. Continuing dependence – technical, economic, cultural, sometimes even political – on more advanced countries is inescapable. A few people in the newly sovereign countries accept a degree of dependence as a necessary price of progress, especially if it benefits them personally. But many emotionally resent it. When a number of small and underdeveloped countries depend in this way largely on a single great and highly industrialized power, it is convenient to speak of an imperial system. Such systems may grow up from the devolution of colonial empires into communities and commonwealths, which maintain an attenuated version of the economic and other links that existed in colonial times; or they may grow up from gradual penetration of an adjacent and underdeveloped area, as has happened with the US in the Caribbean. The economic links tend to include tied currencies, tariff and quota protection, and a guaranteed market for most of the client states' exports (often a single product in oversupply in the world market). The imperial government shares with the private sector of its economy in varying proportions the responsibility for providing development capital and other forms of investment, and for training such local specialists as are required (and their number rises as all production, including agriculture, becomes more technical and more complex). The imperial power also provides some administrative stiffening, a cultural and educational stimulus, and perhaps an impulse towards improved social services.

Such imperial systems run counter to the prevailing political philosophy of a post-colonial world administered by a large number of independent, equal and sovereign governments. Their competence and moral structure varies as enormously as the territorial extent, population and stage of development of the 'nations' they rule and represent. But it is taken for granted that the governments and politically conscious citizens of most nations – especially those formerly subject to alien rule – should cherish their national sovereignty. They regard it as a natural aim to make their independence more absolute and to increase their economic and cultural self-sufficiency. Even the most seemingly logical federal aspirations are apt to founder on this rock.

The recognition and understanding of imperial systems is also made more difficult by the fact that they are usually mentioned in public only by their opponents. It is a field in which absurd and passionate exaggerations easily distort a limited reality. A whole mythology of 'neo-colonialism' and 'exploitation' is based on the premise that an imperial relationship works only to the disadvantage of the underdeveloped client states. Those who appreciate the benefits that can be conferred, whether spokesmen for imperial governments and corporations or citizens of the client states, tend to minimize the significance of the relationship or even to pretend that it does not exist. Of course an imperial system will contain some element of exploitation and certainly brings some compensating advantages to the imperial power in return for its outlay of resources and effort. Otherwise such systems would not come into being. But the advantages to the client states, or at any rate their citizens, are proportionally much greater when measured by objective criteria. Indeed the imperial relationship often provides these communities with an economic and administrative 'windbreak' which is almost indispensable. This windbreak could be provided by a more diffused system of support at considerably greater effort and cost, and some gain in 'national dignity'.

(This is not the place to consider the wider implications of the conflict between imperial systems and the aspirations of national sovereignty. But one or two questions may be noted in passing. For instance, what is the value to mankind in general, and to the inhabitants of small backward states in particular, of making more absolute the sovereignty of micro-national states? Who in the small states exercises political independence – in other words, how large is the decision-making group? What can be done to give the representatives of client states a greater say in determining the policies of the imperial system that most directly affect their interests? What are the prospects of replacing existing relationships by a more diffused system, equally effective, more costly and more emotionally acceptable?)

There are growing resemblances between these Western patterns and the Soviet imperial system. These are likely to be obscured by the major differences, espcially on the political plane, and by the truly exploitative policy of Stalin's impoverished Soviet state towards the territories it occupied at the end of World War II. These resemblances and differences are particularly relevant to Cuba, whose rulers have in effect opted out of one system into the other.

It is also worth noting in the Cuban and Caribbean context that in theory an economic and strategic imperium of the United States or Soviet kind, that encompasses a system of politically independent states with a minimum [which in the Soviet case amounts to a great deal] of interference in their internal political autonomy, provides in a natural way for its own devolution as and when the client national states are able to assume greater responsibilities on their own.

In practice it often happens that the economy of the [imperial] system becomes more complex and more integrated, that technological advances in production move ever further ahead of local capacity, and that social expectations rise. The result is that both the economic and the political systems of the micro-national states become less able to achieve adequate standards on their own, outside the imperium, however great the political desire for greater independence may be. For a small and underdeveloped state without exceptional natural resources to disengage itself from dependence on an imperium and to rely on a more diffused system of support, a conscious policy decision by the imperial power and large injections of aid from other sources are usually necessary. This is especially the case if material and social standards are not to fall.

The imperial relationship between the United States and the independent countries bordering on the Caribbean has brought striking benefits to them, notably increased material wealth and the diffusion of modern technology. But inevitably it stimulates development along certain lines rather than others; and this development, along with the very nature and mode of operation of an imperial economic system, cause special stresses and problems. This is the familiar predicament of states that are politically independent but whose economies form subordinate parts of a larger whole over which they have in practice little or no control. In the American case in particular the main stimulus is exerted not so much by the actions of the United States government, which prefers to respect political independence wherever it reasonably can, as by private economic and other enterprise. And there is no need to accept dogmas about 'exploitation' to recognize that the pressures of free competition, in the Caribbean as elsewhere, tend to discourage private companies from assuming the social responsibilities that it is normally the duty of the state to provide, but which many Caribbean governments are too weak or too irresponsible to organize and pay for.

In countries where an educated commercial and professional class is fostered by a special relationship to the imperial power, large elements and perhaps the majority of that class may come to see greater advantage to themselves in practice – economic and also intellectual and cultural – in continuing to develop the country within the framework of the imperium rather than in its narrowly conceived interests as a micronational state. Their rejection of parochial economic loyalties is often only half-conscious, and is matched by a parallel assimilation of the values of the imperium. This had already happened to the wealthy criollo aristocracy of Cuba in the nineteenth century. After 1898 the island became more North American than anywhere outside United States and Canadian jurisdiction. In the case of Cuba, moreover, the upper and middle classes included substantial numbers of first- or second-generation immigrants from Spain and elsewhere, attracted by the opportunities there after independence. Many of these people, anxious to better themselves and ready to accept change, learnt English and accepted North American values, and acquired their professional and technical training in the United States. This was true of the upper and middle class generally to such an extent that the Cuba which inspired their loyalty was not an independent and essentially inward-looking micro-national state but rather a differentiated (and of course politically autonomous) member of a wider economic and cultural system. So too, for instance, those for whom Senghor speaks in Senegal look to France, notwithstanding their newly won nationhood, as the source of much of their culture, their technology and their economic livelihood.

The trouble is that when an economy and its dominant classes are increasingly absorbed into a wider system in this way, a conflict of loyalties and even a spiritual vacuum is apt to develop. In the argument about how far an economy can, or should, accept integration into a wider system in which it has little say, round what can the wider aspirations of man crystallize? Patriotic and national sentiment in particular, which most men feel and the ruling classes of the small states respect and sometimes idealize, is wounded and unsatisfied. It is difficult for some people to transfer loyalty to something wider than their own national community, especially if this wider grouping is not officially recognized and their community occupies a subordinate position in it. This wounding of patriotic sentiment is usually felt most keenly by two groups. The first is the traditional leaders of small states, notably the officers of the armed forces; and the second is the intelligentsia, whether they are loyal to traditional ideas or have been trained and formed by the imperial system, whether they are Marxist or not. This conflict of loyalties arises even when the material benefits of association are large.

This wounding of patriotic – or one may say micro-national – sentiment is apt to fuse with the social discontent and aspirations of those towards the bottom of the social scale who may have benefited relatively less from the imperial relationship, and whose expectations may have risen faster than their material benefits. When this happens, an explosive mixture is created.[2] This is the case even though it is noteworthy that the discontent of the less-privileged classes and races is often largely passive and is stirred up or simply postulated by the 'revolutionary elite'.

THE PROBLEM OF MINISTATES

The previous section was written thirty years ago. In 1967, shortly after I returned to London I wrote a paper for the British Committee for the Theory of International Politics on the wider aspects of the Cuban Revolution.[3] The excerpt above sets out the problems of size and adequacy as they appeared to me at the height of the decolonization process. Most of it seems to me still valid: surprisingly, because so much has changed in other aspects of the international scene. Most conspicuously, the question still remains of a status for ministates, in which local loyalties can find a reasonably comfortable place.

Ministates, microstates and what Robert Jackson in his admirable analysis calls quasi-states[4] are rather unsatisfactory shorthand terms for those small states which because of their inadequate size, stage of development and experience are in practice client or subordinate political entities. The degree of dependence varies, of course; it is not a question of drawing a line but of recognizing a category. The ministates do not merely have varying degrees of local autonomy: they are formally independent, especially in ceremonial and symbolic contexts, and have seats on the appropriate omnilateral bodies. But their independence is not something that they can sustain for themselves (as developed small states like Singapore and Luxembourg can); it is dependent on a substantial infusion of various kinds of outside assistance. The awareness of this situation produces the conflict of loyalties mentioned in the passage above. A disturbingly large number of the supposedly equal members of our international society come under the heading of ministates. To recognize that their function in the international system is different from that of the United States or Singapore is a step, perhaps a necessary step, towards finding a more satisfying place in international society for ministates. A satisfying role needs to acknowledge and indeed foster their formal independence and self-reliance, and to develop a sense of partnership with the sources of aid. But the ministates need to accept an outside say in their domestic affairs. And we all need to recognize that states with different structures, especially economic structures, have different functions in world society.

We also need to find a more self-respecting place in international society for autonomous entities to which for various practical reasons it is difficult to accord full independent statehood with the present connotations of that status. Examples are the Palestinians, the Bosnian Serbs, the Cypriot Turks, the Sri Lanka Tamils, and many other groups. The wide gap in nominal status between the autonomous

entities and the theoretically independent ministates does not correspond with reality. Autonomous but formally not independent political entities are also in a sense quasi-states. They should have a more
recognized international status, without having to accord them full
sovereignty. We could then make a less absolute distinction between
them and highly dependent but nominally sovereign ministates. The
hegemonial donors and international organizations could treat both
categories in practice in much the same way. Many problems,
especially those of nationalism and pride, of receipt of aid, and of
ensuring human rights, would be eased if a more pragmatic view of
the functions of the two categories came to be generally recognized.

However, there is one important difference between the two categories. The dependent states created by the Europeans achieved independence while retaining the areas of jurisdiction assigned to them by
the colonial administrators. That is clearly not the same thing as ethnic
self-determination. The westernized ruling elites in the newly independent states much dislike the general principle of self-determination.
It can also be applied to ethnic and other local majorities which the
Europeans had not found it convenient to set up as separate dependencies, and might therefore subtract populations and territories from the
jurisdiction of the new states. Indeed if self-determination for ethnic
identities were restored to the legitimacy which it enjoyed in the
1920s, and were insisted on by the hegemonial powers, many of
the newly independent states would disintegrate. Even without the
endorsement of a right to self-determination, some of the ethnic or
other identities which were not accorded separate dependent statehood
by the European colonizers, and to which self-determination therefore
did not apply in the heady days of decolonization, became areas of
trouble. Katanga and the Tutsi areas of Zaire, Biafra in Nigeria,
Unita in Angola are the most conspicuous examples of a host of
ethnic entities that a little international encouragement would bring
to the surface. The Tamils of Sri Lanka, the Turkish Cypriots, the
Kurds, the Kashmiri Muslims and the Chechens are similar prominent
examples elsewhere. It is a testimony to the solidity and the relevance
to local conditions of the dependent territorial jurisdictions set up by
the Europeans, that in spite of the ethnic problems their new rulers
have ensured that they remain almost exactly the same as in imperial
times.

In fact it has suited both the new ruling elites and the industrially
developed donor powers to continue the investment and the administrative and technical underpinning of the newly independent states.
The donor states and their corporations have the same interest in

the products, the labour and the markets of the new states, the same interest in order and security, and the same humanitarian impulses, as before: but in a more generalized way than when colonies belonged to individual empires. The concern of the developed North for the welfare of the ex-colonies has extended from *raison d'état* or *raison d'empire* to *raison de système*. The broadened responsibility takes account of the important difference that trade, investment and administrative underpinning by donors (including international agencies like the World Bank) now require the consent and co-operation of the rulers of the newly independent states.

Some new rulers, and their sympathizers elsewhere, have developed a rhetoric of the 'development entitlement' of impoverished countries, of inter-state distributive justice, and of rights which seem to be defined by adverse circumstances. That is understandable special pleading. But there is not a single pool of wealth in a single global economy. The developed economies can, and do, produce more wealth in the ministates by making investment, technology and markets available. Some of the additional wealth will remain in the ministates: how much will depend on the bargains which those states make with the international organizations, individual donor states and private corporations involved.

The non-settler dependent states which the Europeans constructed were designed to function economically and strategically as parts of an imperial whole. Their internal structure, the ultimate shape into which they were supposed to grow, were set by the imperial power. The imperial authorities were responsible for a range of standards of European civilization. The range ran from law and order and safety for economic enterprises, which had motivated the Europeans to set up the dependent states in the first place, through standards of literacy and health to commercial law and human rights. Where the imperial power was a democracy, it was held accountable by public opinion 'at home'; and in any case increasingly by the rest of the international society. These European creations, now decolonized, are often (especially in Africa) ethnically arbitrary but administratively reasonable, or have been made so by the European state-builders. It is these states, and these configurations, that are protected by the new legitimacy of independence and the shield of collective economic and territorial security for former colonial states.

TWO IMPERIAL SYSTEMS

Let us now turn to two specific groups of newly independent states.

The **American imperial system** covering most of the island states of the Caribbean and the smaller Central American republics has been made clearer by the events of the last thirty years. The disparity of size, wealth and technical competence between the great republic and the ministates to its south gives the United States a position that it does not have in South America or any longer in Mexico. US imperial authority has made itself felt in the ministate area to its south since the end of last century, when it created the Republic of Panama and helped Cuba to independence from Spain. Woodrow Wilson reconciled his belief in self-determination and neutrality with his military interventions in Mexico, Haiti, the Dominican Republic and Nicaragua. Most recently, armed American interventions in Grenada, Panama and Haiti have affirmed the imperial power's right and responsibility to ensure that those ministates are governed in ways and by leaders acceptable to the imperial power. Such operations are carried out with a figleaf of international approval and a small participation by other states, preferably those in the imperium. But nobody doubts that the decisions about what to do, and how, and why, are taken in the United States. In parallel with US interventions are the less conspicuous forms of inducement to achieve the imperial power's purposes in other Central American and Caribbean states. Both are primarily designed to promote Western standards of civilization, human rights and democracy; and they cost the imperial power more than the protection of direct US interests brings in return.

The most important, continuous and general ties of the imperium are economic. The small states receive special privileges in the vast US market both for their dominant product such as sugar, and also for the products of small industries which help to wean their economies from excessive dependence on a single crop. The ministates also benefit from a wide variety of aid and technical programmes, some channelled through omnilateral organizations like the World Bank but largely at US prompting and with US money.

The US imperial dominion in the Caribbean and Central America is disliked by the larger, less-dominated South American republics and by Mexico. For this reason, and because the imperial policy costs money, and also because it goes against the US belief in independence, the imperium and especially military intervention are opposed by large segments of US public opinion, and their reluctance is reflected in the Legislature. Of course the policy brings benefits to the imperial power. The obvious purpose during the cold war was to keep the Soviets out of the area, or at least limited to Cuba. But the same policies continue since the demise of the Soviet Union. Other advantages are the promotion of private enterprise, control of the drug traffic and stemming the flood of illegal immigrants. Thus the imperium brings benefits to both sides. The relationship does not exclude the small states from obtaining minor economic and technical advantages from other sources like Europe, the Commonwealth and Japan, so long as these do not interfere with what might be called US suzerainty.

The United States has traditionally looked at the whole western hemisphere, the area protected by the Monroe Doctrine, as a region from which it is entitled to exclude any undue influence from the Old World. In the hemisphere the Great Good Neighbour has also assumed the right to influence the policies of the South American republics where it can, in order to protect its interests and to promote its principles. The US ambassador to a major South American state told me recently that he was under considerable pressure from the Congress in Washington to get the local government to act on 'the three D's': debt, drugs and democracy. South American governments recognize the first two subjects as legitimate, but (unlike many of their subjects) resent US pressure on their domestic freedom of action. The combined weight of the South American countries together is often enough to balance US power on such issues. But it is notable that they have recently moved a considerable distance towards US standards of democracy and fiscal responsibility.

Tropical Africa is a somewhat different case. Though there are a few European settlers, the independent states that now compose that area are European creations governed by Western-educated Africans. Before the area was divided up into states on European lines, the population consisted largely of various sedentary and nomadic tribal peoples, whose loyalties did not go beyond their ethnic boundaries. The governing elites of the newly independent states have undertaken the task of moulding the peoples in their jurisdiction into nations, whose primary loyalty would be to the state. European nationalists wanted every nation to have its own state, supposing the nation, the Volk, to be already in existence. In many of the new independences it is a case of every state needing to create a nation. Tribal loyalties remain strong in tropical Africa. But now Africans have that new thing a state, governed by people like them; the sense of belonging to the state is growing.

Many of the recently independent African states are not ministates in size. Nigeria probably has a population of over 100 million. But they share some problems with ministates. Most Africans who are aware of statehood are not (as I see it) animated by nationalist passion for their state, as Europeans were and some still are. The passion where it exists is still tribal; and it threatens domestic rather than international order. Rwanda–Burundi, Liberia, Sierra Leone and Somalia are only the conspicuous recent malignancies in a very general and usually more benign pattern. The state is apt to be a second tier of loyalty, muted by a spreading concern about the competence of the independent regimes: an awareness of how difficult it is for the states inherited from the European colonizers to manage on their own. A growing proportion of the citizens-in-the-making recognize, in addition to their ethnic and state allegiances, their dependence on aid from outside. That dependence is not only economic: it is apt to include some protection for the aspiring citizenry against the government of their own state.

The Lomé aid agreements and other links to the European Union help the new states to spread their dependence, and their markets, wider than the former colonial power. Aid from omnilateral organizations like the World Bank and from the United States also plays a significant part; as does aid from Commonwealth and rich Islamic countries. Yet links to the former colonial power, rooted in familiarity, remain. Indeed French-speaking tropical Africa – *la Francophonie africaine* – still has the main characteristics of an imperium. France is the leading donor, especially in the military field, and in most states underwrites the currency and higher education. The French government intervenes with armed force where it considers necessary, as the United States does in and around the Caribbean. France helps more than other former imperial powers to maintain the functioning integrity of the African states which it created, and systematically uses its aid and other forms of pressure to coax the governments of those states towards more democracy and human rights, or in other words back towards the Western standards of civilization which it gradually introduced in colonial times. British governments and public opinion feel less obligation in Africa for a number of reasons. Britain still continues to do much in Africa, especially in the fields of education and technical assistance, and uses its influence in favour of the same standards of civilization. But the relationship is no longer imperial.

In the general pattern of dependence the imperial systems of individual powers described above come somewhere between the overt and formal dependence of colonial empires and the collective hegemonial relation of the donor powers to nominally sovereign recipient states. It is instructive to compare them with the independent client states of Germany and Italy which once formed part of the French and Austrian imperial systems in Europe, mentioned in Chapter 2.

The US and French imperial systems seem to be moving away from overt mono-imperial control towards a more collective authority. The provision of the wide range of aid, and the enforcement of the conditions attached to it, are likely to become more diffused, more costly and more emotionally acceptable, as suggested in my paper. But the extent of dependence will not be lessened thereby. It is misleading to limit the term dependence to dependence on a single power.

CHANGING CONCEPTS OF SOVEREIGNTY

In the West, practitioners and academics alike have growing doubts about the continued relevance of sovereign statehood, or at least the need to be bound by it. (These doubts go back a long way. There is an immense literature on the subject, and on functional and other alternatives to 'the nation–state' and to independent statehood generally.) External and internal independence no longer seems to be a monolithic whole, but rather a set of areas of action which used to come tied in a package or bundle, but can be separated. The different areas of action – such as defense, the economy and human rights – can be transferred to various confederal institutions, as we noted in Europe in Chapter 2. Or smaller states can administer them in accordance with the prescriptions of omnilateral bodies like the UN or the World Bank (which in practice means the collective hegemony of the great powers). In either case decisions in these areas can be partially or wholly removed from the jurisdiction of a state government without destroying the identity of the state. If I may quote from my *Evolution of International Society*,

> to put it more prosaically, the modern successors of the European princes find themselves constrained by the pressures of a tightening system and by the institutions and practices of a more integrated society to act increasingly in ways that deprive them of independence de facto, externally and internally . . . while leaving intact the symbolic legitimacy of the state and varying degrees of real autonomy.[5]

Independence for ex-colonial states able to stand on their own feet is clearly desirable at present, within the limits that apply to all states. We may conclude that it is on balance a useful though sometimes rather fictitious status even for those which are not. It gratifies national pride and individual self-respect. It assuages the conflict of loyalties that haunts the Western-educated elites. By removing a motive for rebellion it works in favour of peace and order. On a more practical level independence helps small weak states to diversify their dependence from a single imperial master. Where collective imperial authority is exercised in practice, that authority is less conspicuous and less irritating, though ministates which are dependent on a single imperial power find themselves in much the same position as before.

Of course there is a price to be paid for nominal independence where it cannot yet be made a reality. That price is not paid by the developed states of the world, which taken together get most of what they want for less money and effort. The chief sufferers are the largely illiterate majorities in the less developed newly independent states. There individual prosperity, health, justice and personal freedom are all too often less than they were at the time of decolonization. The beneficiaries are the administrative and military elites, whose efforts achieved independence. Hegemonial 'neo-colonial' authority mitigates to some extent the price that individuals in dependent states pay for independence, while enhancing the benefits. But outside Asia the price remains high.

NOTES

1 Claude, Inis, 'Myths about the State', *Review of International Studies*, vol. 12, 1986, pp. 1–2.
2 It is significant that Fidel Castro, who owes much to Mussolini and the Spanish Falange as well as to Communism, chose as the slogan of his revolution '*Patria o muerte*'.
3 Text available in the library of the Royal Institute of International Affairs, St James's Square, London SW1.
4 See Robert H. Jackson, *Quasi-states: Sovereignty, international relations and the Third World*, Cambridge University Press, 1990, especially pp. 21–31. This book is the best discussion of the subject I have seen.
5 Adam Watson, *The Evolution of International Society*, Routledge, 1992, p. 307.

5 Standards of civilization and human rights

Human rights is now such a topical subject that it is virtually impossible to keep up with the flood of literature which it has generated. This chapter is limited to one aspect, the clash of legitimacies between independence and international responsibility for human rights, as it affects the freedom of action of governments.[1]

On the one hand sovereign independence is not something marginal or contingent: it is, as explained earlier, the constituent legitimacy of our contemporary international society. On the other hand the Western concept of human rights assumes that 'the international community' has the right, and indeed the moral obligation, to denounce or take action against states that flout the human rights of their subjects.

Since World War II sovereign independence has been regarded as the only internationally acceptable status for a state. But the rich and powerful highly developed states do not regard this status as conferring on the rulers and governments of other states a license to behave as they like, either externally or internally. In the last chapter we saw that small and newly independent states especially need so much from the rest of the world that the rich powers are well placed to bring economic and other inducements to bear on the domestic policies of weaker states. The great powers are not only interested in those standards of civilization which protect their own economic interests. They also feel a responsibility for those standards of civilized government which protect the rights of the governed against their rulers.

STATEHOOD AND AUTHORITY

Independence, and the corollary of no outside interference, were the cardinal emotion and dogma of the anti-colonial movement. The anti-colonial elites aimed to take over the dependent states with their machinery of government and their existing boundaries but free of imperial control. What the local elites wanted was to acquire sovereignty for themselves in the name of their state.

The leaders of colonial independence movements, whether 'settlers' or 'natives', have all had this aim. It was the purpose of the 'founding fathers' who organized the secessions of the thirteen British colonies in North America and the Spanish American colonies; as it was the purpose of those who took over the Asian dependencies of the Europeans, the ethnically very arbitrary dependent states created by the European colonial powers in Africa, and the fairly arbitrary non-Russian 'republics' of the Soviet Union.

Even if we leave aside the question of preventive intervention in which a dictator or ruling group makes obvious preparations to invade a neighbour, in my experience none of the new governments resulting from decolonization expected, or even seriously asserted, that there should never be outside intervention or pressure to modify internal misgovernment however outrageous. Almost all the new rulers admitted when challenged that there would be cases extreme enough to justify international economic sanctions.[2] They might agree that perhaps, if sanctions did not work, forceful intervention might be necessary as a last resort. But certainly all that did not apply, in the eyes of the new governments, to what one might call routine abuses of human rights. Indeed, for an ex-colonial power like Britain or France to raise such hypothetical questions made the governments of the newly independent states suspicious that the powerful blocs from which they wanted to be non-aligned would use such arguments as pretexts for neo-colonial intervention.

I understand that the opinions of these governments have not changed much since. But in recent years human rights have assumed greater importance as an international issue then they had in the heyday of decolonization. Most governments find it prudent to proclaim their belief in human rights more emphatically, and also in practice to respect somewhat more the rights of their opponents.

In addition to the desire to preserve as much as possible of their recently acquired or reacquired sovereignty, the governments and ruling elites of most newly independent states are keenly aware of the tenuous nature of their authority, and the difficulty of holding together the machinery of state and the loyalty of the population at all. Most of the rulers and administrators have been trained either in colonial administration, which was more authoritarian than in the mother countries, or in the military which is based on a chain of command. Professor Wallerstein compares the function of government in newly independent states to a surgical clamp, which holds the structure together while new tissues develop and become accepted. Even so Europeanized a leader as President Senghor of Senegal, who had been a minister in French governments, told me that for an African state to become a nation, people needed to have their loyalties focused on the new state and its legitimate chiefs, and that in such states opposition from political parties and the media, seeking to shake the loyalty of the people to the government and to replace it with a rival group, was still too disruptive: in contrast to France and Britain, where public acceptance of governmental authority depended on the ability of the governed to speak freely about the government and to change it when the majority so wished. President Islam Karimov of Uzbekistan recently formulated the issue in general terms: 'Any country needs strong executive power when it gains its own statehood. Strong executive power is necessary to prevent bloodshed and confrontation, and to preserve ethnic and civil concord, peace and stability. . . . It is necessary for the progress of democracy.'

Such statements are justifications by rulers: but they contain a substantial element of truth. In most newly independent states there is a fear of anarchy and a desire for increased security and prosperity; and therefore widespread acquiescence in a degree of authoritarian government and denial of individual human rights, so long as some private economic enterprise is allowed, especially in the production and distribution of food. Nor are such ideas alien to the West. When Hobbes wrote his *Leviathan*, strong executive authority seemed to many preferable to anarchy. It was only in the eighteenth century, when the dangers of anarchy faded, that individual freedoms began to assume the overriding importance which they now have in the West.

Half of the present members of the UN have had little or no previous experience of a modern state where the accepted authority (as opposed to the ability to compel obedience) and the administrative capacity of the government are derived from within the culture. What is learnt from outside one's own cultural tradition carries less conviction in times of stress. The rulers of the ex-colonial states are therefore less willing than Westerners to rely on Western ways of governing and more fearful of the danger of chaos. This is the case even in Asia. For instance the Chinese states (the mainland, Taiwan, Singapore, etc.) do have a millenial tradition of accepted autocracy based on a Son of Heaven and an administrative bureaucracy. The tradition of authority has come down through a century of compulsory obedience to an alternation of warlords and monolithic party rule in China itself, and colonial rule elsewhere. The governments of Chinese states, and most of the population, assume a much greater degree of authority than Western societies now find acceptable, and they tend to consider political democracy and Western-style human rights a threat to the stability of their states, in a way that private economic enterprise is not. Mao Tse-dung late in his life thought the greatest danger facing China was a relapse into chaos.

The case of Beijing China is particularly significant in the context of human rights. Communist China has a bad human rights record by Western standards. It also has a veto in the Security Council of the UN; and since Chinese approval or acquiescence is necessary for any action under UN auspices, it is the power that modifies and sets limits to action the Western powers may wish to take through the UN. It is also a power whose active co-operation is needed on many international issues, and whose rapidly growing economy makes economic sanctions against it impracticable. China is a major piece on the chessboard. Western governments do not have a free hand in formulating a China policy; they are constrained by the need to weigh a complex balance of advantage and feasibility.

In the UN China is a leading defender of the sovereignty of other states and opponent of interference in their internal affairs. So is the other population giant, India, though it is a democracy opposed to China on many other issues. These two states, that comprise about two-fifths of the world's population, and the many other states which support them, play down the legitimacy of international concern for the human rights of individual citizens against their own government. They prefer to stress the collective rights of the peoples or races in whose name they claim to speak.

Many states proceed from the demand for equality for all races to a demand, or plea, for more egalitarian distribution of purchasing power regardless of where the wealth is produced. The demand for 'economic justice' is supported by the standards of living provisions of the Universal Declaration on Human Rights, discussed below. But a number of Asian states from Taiwan and Singapore to Kuwait have much higher levels of well-being than world averages, and would suffer from a truly egalitarian redistribution. Such states are usually less willing than Western states to assume the obligations of donors, or to hand over part of their wealth to others whom they regard as less industrious and thrifty.

THE EXTENSION OF STANDARDS OF CIVILIZATION

All this does not mean that international pressure for better observance of human rights is ineffective. On the contrary. Seen in historical perspective, the economic and similar pressures which the governments of the industrialized West bring to bear on other states, in order to make them implement individual human rights formulated by the West, are part of the general effort by the West to induce the rest of the world to conform to Western standards of civilization. The process is also part of the gradual erosion of sovereign statehood and of the rule established by the European princes against interference in each other's internal affairs. Both are significant trends in the functioning of our present international society.

Human rights have a long and respectable history in the West. We can leave aside the campaigns of the French revolutionaries for '*les droits de l'homme*'[3] which were not endorsed by the rest of the European international society. We can begin with the formal outlawing of the slave trade in the Vienna settlement of 1815, at British initiative. It took some time, and a considerable amount of interference by the British and other navies with shipping on the high seas, to end the trade; but the international legitimation of the principle by its promulgation in a treaty, and its acceptance by the leading European powers, greatly assisted the task.

Similarly in 1884–85 the Congress of Berlin formulated the international obligation of colonial powers to act as trustees for the welfare and advancement of primitive and dependent peoples. This obligation was made more specific in the League of Nations mandates after World War I, and by the trusteeship provisions of the United Nations. It is sometimes said, especially by those who consider it correct to paint all colonial activity as exploitation, that the colonizing powers disregarded these pious resolutions. Certainly colonial practice on the ground found these principles as often 'honoured in the breach as in the observance'. But it made a significant difference that the principles were declared by the colonizing governments to be their policies, and publicly so proclaimed in the territories themselves.

In fact ideas about the rights of man and of dependent peoples were established as international obligations by the European governments, reflecting 'progressive' public opinion in their societies and in the West generally. They formed a significant part of the **standards of civilization**, which Western governments set up during the brief period of European domination of the world, both to bridle themselves and to impose on all other governments. Geritt Gong's book

The Standard of Civilization in International Society illustrates the gap between the principle and the practice of the Western powers, particularly in China. Even so, the concept of standards of civilized behaviour steadily modified the practice of governments, both Western and non-Western, towards their citizens and subject peoples. The principles and standards were proclaimed by Western governments to be of universal validity, but they grew out of the matrix of Western culture, and were perceived as such even by those non-Western governments and peoples that espoused them, from the King of Siam to Sorbonne-educated Africans.

The same is true of the set of principles and ideals now bracketed together as **human rights.** The Universal Declaration on the subject issued by the General Assembly of the UN on December 10, 1948 under American leadership, covers a range of rights which can be divided for our purposes into two broad categories. The first category is designed to protect the individual from what may be called the arbitrary exercise of authority by his/her own government. It includes freedom of speech and opinion, personal security, due judicial process, freedom from racial and religious discrimination, and other restraints on governmental action. These are limitations which governments can (other circumstances permitting) ensure to the governed, though perhaps at considerable risk to themselves and to order in a new or fragile state. But the Universal Declaration also asserts a second category, the rights of everyone to many desirable things which few if any governments can ensure: for instance its often quoted Article 25 states that 'everyone has the right to a standard of living adequate for the health and well-being of himself and his family [no feminist drafting in 1948], including food, clothing, housing and medical care, and necessary social services' etc. This category is couched, so to speak, not in the formula 'Thou the government shalt not', but 'Thou the government shalt'.

Now if the Universal Declaration merely means that all these desirable things, from freedom of the press to 'necessary' social services, are rights in the same self-evident sense as liberty and the pursuit of happiness – that is, rights which we should all work towards and which will be realized some day but not overnight, rights that Jefferson who coined the formula did not take to mean that he and his colleagues needed to free their slaves – then few governments have any great difficulty with the Declaration, or any real cause to denounce other governments for failing to implement it. Demands for implementation can be left to monitoring organizations like Amnesty International, political oratory and the Western media.

Many of the governments in whose names the Declaration was signed, or which have subscribed to it since, scarcely took it seriously. One could not object to such platitudinous ideas, and one could always say later that one was doing one's best. Nevertheless there is an awesome cynicism about Stalin's assent. No doubt Hitler would have cheerfully signed too, if it had suited him. Does not the refrain of the Horst Wessel song proclaim '*Der Tag für Freiheit und für Brot bricht an*' – the day for freedom and for bread is here?

But several governments, and particularly the government of the United States, the only state with a global reach, are inclined to treat the Universal Declaration, and even more so the Helsinki Agreement on human rights in Europe, as if they are contracts or treaty obligations. In other words such declarations are held to represent not signposts or a 'goal-seeking framework' but legally binding commitments. According to this interpretation, other governments can be held to be in breach of them, and can legitimately be induced to implement them by the use of the carrot and the stick. The US government for instance has human rights officers in its embassies abroad, who report on the implementation of these rights (paying more attention to some than others) and a global report is then submitted to the Congress each year. Aid can then be increased or diminished to improve implementation; and trade facilities like most-favoured nation treatment can be witheld.

In his latest book, *Around the Cragged Hill*, George Kennan compares the current American attitude to human rights to that of a century ago with regard to China.

> You had an example of the satisfaction many of us Americans derived from demanding of other governments policies consistent with what we liked to believe to be our own cherished national virtues, even when there was no serious prospect that the other powers in question would or could do what we were demanding of them, and even – in some instances – when we ourselves had no very serious intention of living up to these same demands. In many American minds, the mere fact that we had stated these admirable principles, and had demanded respect for them, and had done so in ways that would allow our government to appear in noble posture before world and American opinion, was felt to be quite enough. Whether any actual good came, or could have come, from this demand was beside the point. . . . I sense a certain whiff of this same sanctimoniousness in American statements and demands about human rights.

The Western sense that standards of civilization and human rights in non-Western countries are inadequate, and Western misgivings like Kennan's about such criticism, go a long way back into the nineteenth century. Wilkie Collins, in a passage stiff with irony in *The Woman in White*, written about 1860, has the rascally Italian count say, 'Here in England there is one virtue. And there, in China, there is another virtue. And John Englishman says my virtue is the genuine virtue. And John Chinaman says my virtue is the genuine virtue.' The heroine answers in terms that are still in use about the recent suppression of dissidence in Tienanmen Square,

> Surely we have one unquestionable virtue in England which is wanting in China. The Chinese authorities kill thousands of innocent people on the most frivolous pretexts. We in England are free from all guilt of that kind – we commit no such dreadful crime – we abhor reckless bloodshed with all our hearts.

To which the bad count replies,

> Yes, I agree with her. John Bull does abhor the crimes of John Chinaman. He is the quickest old gentleman at finding out faults that are his neighbours', and the slowest old gentleman at finding out faults that are his own.

EFFECTS OF PRESSURE FOR HUMAN RIGHTS

How much effect does such governmental pressure have, and at what price in other fields of the management of international relations? Even George Kennan[4] acknowledges that US insistence on human rights, and willingness to accept disadvantages to other US interests in order to promote them, has been beneficial to their observance. Indeed I do not think this can be reasonably denied. Governments and public opinion everywhere are in fact being induced to accept Western standards in these matters, and increasingly to implement them; just as they were induced to accept and implement Western standards on such issues as slavery and trusteeship. As Galileo said, '*Eppur si muove*'.

The considerable impact of Western and especially American efforts to promote both categories of human rights (thou the government shalt not and thou the government shalt) has been greatly augmented in the last few years by the collapse of the Soviet and other Communist tyrannies. But as the Red Queen explained to Alice, in this backsliding, looking-glass world you have to run a good deal faster than Alice was running, even to stay where you are. The population explosion increases the population of states with poor records in the second category of human rights, which are often also the states with the worst records in the first category, relative to the prosperous industrial democracies. Freedom House of New York calculates that in spite of the collapse of Communism the percentage of people living in 'free societies' has declined from 36 per cent in 1983 to 25 per cent in 1993. While such precision about such a nebulous set of criteria is suspect, the general point is well taken. The executive director of Amnesty International says more simply 'Things are worse'. They would be worse still if Western governments had not pressed other governments towards better observance.

To establish which human rights the West is promoting in this way, and at what price, we must leave generalizations, and look at a long list of specific cases: each case is more complex than the single-issue advocates of either sovereignty or human rights would have us believe. As the French Minister of Foreign Affairs recently observed: 'To oversimplify a problem is not to solve it.' What Professor John Vincent called 'the diplomacy of justice' has to weigh each tangle of issues separately, and then all of them together, which is more than this paper can attempt. However, a few illustrations may be useful.

Some of the complexities in the case of **China** were noted above. The carrot of drawing the present government of China gradually into a partnership in the management of international society (which that government hankers after and is now a stated goal of US policy) would produce considerable gains in various fields, but it would also reinforce the principles of sovereignty and non-interference which that government champions. The stick of trade sanctions would be partially successful at best. Sanctions would hinder the economic growth which is bringing to the population, especially of South China, the benefits listed in Article 25 of the Universal Declaration, even though political freedoms are denied. How damaging is it to the diplomacy of human rights elsewhere in the world to recognize, tacitly, that some powers, like China and formerly the Soviet Union, are too big and too ruthless for other governments to intervene effectively in their internal affairs?

By contrast, the pressures exerted by the international community on the states of **Subsaharan Africa** have been somewhat more successful in moving those governments to a greater observance of Western standards of civilization. The most conspicuous case is South Africa, where the sticks of sanctions and boycotts, and the subsequent carrots, have helped materially to persuade the white communities to surrender their monopoly of political power. There the crucial issue is whether a transfer of power to the present leaders of the African majority will produce a net gain in either of the two categories of human rights. The present prospects are encouraging. But in other African countries such as Somalia, Liberia and Rwanda, where international military forces have intervened, continued pressure and intervention will be necessary after the troops have departed, if standards of human rights acceptable to the West are to prevail. The same is true of other situations outside Africa, like Cambodia and Bosnia.

A third set of examples involves a range of states from **Peru** to some ex-**Soviet** republics. In Peru President Fujimori did not act according to Western standards of democracy, and the United States imposed mild sanctions on him for that. But greater involvement by foreign powers would be necessary to ensure that full political freedoms in the government-controlled areas of Peru did not provide such opportunities to terrorist guerrillas as to result in a net loss of human rights. The same is true of Tajikstan, and several other states. The Russian government has proclaimed its obligation to intervene in other states of its former empire to protect the rights of minorities.

Occasionally a government violates human rights so scandalously that intervention by a single foreign power, even the former colonial authority, becomes internationally acceptable. French intervention in Bokassa's Central African Empire was largely though not entirely to protect human rights there, including the right not to be killed and eaten by your head of state.

The balance of advantage of any given degree of outside intervention in this or that state, both to human rights in the state concerned and to the legitimacy of the international order, is thus hard to calculate. But as the world becomes more interdependent, pressure by Western and other like-minded governments in favour of human rights is likely to grow, at the expense of what many other governments consider sacrosanct independence. The tightening net of interests and pressures that binds our worldwide system ever more closely together is steadily cracking the walls of sovereignty that separate its member states. The international society that we set up to manage earlier forms of pressure, and which the newly independent states embraced, is therefore finding that its legitimacy is lagging increasingly behind the reality of the tightening net, and of our international practice.

As we saw in the previous chapter, external and internal independence consists of a number of spheres of action which practitioners and academics alike used to think of as bound in a single package.

But it is now clear that the bundle can be separated into its constitutent parts. Consequently, in the West, practitioners and academics alike have growing doubts about the continued relevance of sovereign statehood, or at least the need to be bound by it. The identity of a state, and its nominal independence, can be preserved, while the donors insist on action in areas that particularly concern them, like human rights. They do so directly and through omnilateral bodies like the UN or the World Bank: which in practice means the collective hegemony of the great powers. This one aspect of the wider reality that nation states that are the modern successors of the European princes find themselves constrained to act increasingly in ways that limit their independence *de facto*, externally and internally, while leaving intact the symbolic legitimacy of the state and varying degrees of real autonomy.

The area of sovereignty in which the rulers and governments of new and weak states are most willing to accept hegemonial interference is the economy. They urgently need aid. The donors and the international organizations which they control link the aid to stipulations about how the recipient economy is to be run, which seems to recipient governments understandable, though not always welcome. Aid is intended *inter alia* to improve the material conditions of the population in recipient countries – the second category of human rights – and usually does so. But increasingly donor governments link aid and similar advantages to other issues as well, including the first category of human rights. Such non-economic extensions of donor stipulations impose further limits on absolute sovereignty.

Non-economic demands seem to me likely to meet dogged resistance by those governments that cherish their newly won or restored sovereignty. As the non-Western world grows more populous and more economically developed, we must expect the relative influence of the West on it and on international society generally to decline. The diplomacy of justice and sovereignty is likely to be influenced more than at present by Asian ideas – particularly Islamic, Chinese and Indian. In such circumstances action by Western governments to promote human rights in non-Western countries will usually be more successful with the carrot than the stick, and with negotiated and face-saving compromises. Western governments will also come to see more merit in independence and compromise as they resist the demands of the majority of states on such issues as immigration and the transfer of technology.

Broadly speaking therefore, we can see the principle of sovereign statehood and non-interference in internal affairs as an element of the standards of civilization which are a legacy of European expansion. Sovereignty has become the constituent legitimacy of our global international society, especially cherished by the governments of decolonized dependencies. Human rights are another Western standard of conduct, that is still being actively propagated by the West, with some success. The responsibility which Western governments feel for human rights in other states conflicts with the claims of the governments of those states to sovereignty and freedom from neocolonial interference. We can also see Western efforts to ensure the universal observance of human rights as a strand in the tightening net of interdependence that has recently been breaking down the sovereignty formerly held so dear by the West. But it is only one aim, or responsibility, of the Western donors: and takes its place alongside peace and prosperity, and expense, as an element in the compromises that are continually reached and revised. As the population and wealth of some non-Western and particularly Asian states increases faster than the West, their governments are likely to have more influence on the shifting compromises that donors and recipients are able to work out.

NOTES

1 See R. J. Vincent, *Human Rights and International Relations*, Cambridge University Press, 1986; see also D. Newsom (ed.), *The Diplomacy of Human Rights*, University Press of America, 1986.
2 South Africa in the days of apartheid is the prime example. In Africa Sudan, Nigeria and Libya are also currently candidates for economic sanctions.
3 See *inter alia* the chapter on revolutionary diplomacy in James Der Derian's book, *Diplomacy*, Blackwell, 1987.
4 Kennan, op. cit., pp. 71–7.

6 Independence and responsibility

We have seen that the further the legitimacy of a society of states is towards the multiple independences end of the spectrum, and especially the more anarchic in the technical sense its practice is, the more the maintenance of order depends on the most powerful member states conducting their relations with a sense of prudence and moral obligation. In the first half of this century reliance on such voluntary restraints proved altogether inadequate, with disastrous results. A purpose of this book has been to examine what further limits to independence now operate in practice, and whether they are adequate to the task of maintaining economic, strategic and other forms of order in today's continually tightening world system.

In this chapter I want to look further at some implications of the phrase **responsibility in the conduct of international relations** in societies of substantially independent states. We will examine: first, the obligations of states in today's world; second, what is meant by responsible conduct; and third, the special responsibilities that derive from power. In doing so I want to look at what other curbs may be needed to limit the independence of states.

International responsibility in a society of states has many other meanings. For instance rulers or citizens can feel so committed to a set of religious beliefs, or to abstract nouns like democracy, that it seems to them irresponsible to pursue any mundane advantage outside their own state that damages the cause. These meanings of responsibility are relevant to our enquiry insofar as they involve a commitment to override respect for the independence of other states.

OBLIGATIONS OF DEMOCRATIC STATES

Responsibility implies accountability for one's actions, and for their consequences. To whom are states and statesmen in the modern world usually held accountable for actions beyond their own borders? The French scholar Pierre Hassner draws a useful distinction between three concentric circles of obligation for substantially independent democratic states. First a government's responsibilities to the nation or electorate which it represents, which he calls the *contrat social démocratique*. Second the *contrat féodal* or contracts of allegiance that a state makes with allies and treaty partners in an international society of independent states. Third (and the most nebulous though not the least important today) the *contrat tacite*, the unspecified responsibility of every state for the welfare of mankind and the planet as a whole.[1]

OBLIGATIONS TO THE ELECTORATE

The accepted theory of the modern democratic state is that the government should act in accordance with the wishes of the electorate. When framing its external policy, it has a further obligation to ascertain the national **interests**[2] of its electorate, and in legitimate ways to protect and further those interests. So far so good. But the implementation of this theory raises many problems. The voters in a developed democracy are capable, by and large, of judging where their interests lie in domestic matters that come within their direct experience. But we have seen that modern states are inescapably involved with each other in a tightening net made up of the pressures of the states system, the rules of international society and the hegemonial authority of the strongest powers. These external involvements are beyond the direct horizon of the electorate, and they are so complex, and potentially so dangerous, that they cannot safely be determined by public opinion alone. The winds of public sentiment veer and change, when what is usually needed is a steady course. Democratic governments know that they need a great deal of professional diplomatic, economic and military expertise to weigh up the balance of their state's external interests. A state's interests are not always compatible with each other, or with the wishes of the electorate; experts and statesmen often miscalculate in good faith. Statesmanship has been described as the art of reconciling interests, internally and externally.

   States and their citizens have **principles** as well as interests. Democratic theory recognizes the government's obligation to represent the society that elects it, by enunciating and adhering to the society's principles. Many electors today consider that their government should not only preach and practice their principles abroad, but should also use legitimate means of persuasion to induce other governments to practice them too (as discussed in the last chapter). Two difficulties limit the external exercise of power even by a hegemonial government in response to the will of its electorate. The first is that despite the narcissistic belief of electorates that 'foreigners would do well to be more like us', in fact for cultural and other reasons this may not at all be the case. As we saw in Chapter 5, a foreign state may well have solid and objective reasons for refusing to adopt what others recommend, as well as the desire of a ruling group to retain its political power. The second difficulty is that a nation's principles may conflict not only with its interests but with each other, as in the familiar dichotomies between peace and justice and between world order and human rights.

In most developed Western states, and in some others also, a thoughtful minority public opinion favours a foreign policy which looks beyond national interests, often towards rather hazy and idealistic ideas of world government. But on balance the impact of public opinion, moulded by the news media and excited by their presentation of the news, is to push the conduct of foreign policy further towards freedom of action and thus towards the multiple independences end of the spectrum.

The essence of conventional democratic wisdom is that the government should be responsive to the wishes of the electorate, the 'sovereign people'. But like patriotism, democracy is not enough. Other restraints are needed.

Democratic theory assumes sovereign states. It acknowledges that governments should not merely execute the momentary wishes of the majority. They have an obligation to ascertain as best they can the interests of those they represent, and to act accordingly. Governments, the theory says, have a responsibility to work out how the complex bundle of interests and principles may most effectively be served: it recognizes that the significant element in the bundle is the maintenance of adequate international order, including (the theory sometimes acknowledges) the management of inevitable and often unwelcome change. But merely to say that governments have these responsibilities does not solve the problem. Democratic governments must be responsive to the wishes of the voters; in practice, especially in states where polls and referenda influence policy, a government that acts contrary to the will of the voters will not be re-elected. And there's the rub.

We saw in Chapter 2 that the lesson which some Europeans, particularly Germans, have learnt from the devastation of the two great wars is that, at any rate so far as Europe is concerned, there are actions which must be put beyond the power of any state to take, even if the people of that state want to take it, say, in a fit of nationalist frenzy. In other words there must be *limits to the sovereignty of the people,* whatever democratic theory may say. The Kreisau paper said that not only peace but also internal standards of civilization were incompatible with absolute sovereignty.

OBLIGATIONS TO OTHER STATES

In the second circle of **contractual relations** with other governments and institutions in a society of multiple independences, a government's responsibilities are more precisely formulated. The case of alliances is particularly clear. Alliances between independent states are specific contracts made for mutual practical advantage. Allies rely on the commitments they have received from each other, and reshape their defence arrangements and their foreign policies accordingly; so that allies assume a moral obligation to each other to carry out their share of the bargain in good faith. Alliances are merely particularly clear examples. The same obligation is present in general treaties like the Covenant of the League and the UN Charter, and to a lesser extent in all international contracts.[3] As a general rule, not to carry out a contract, or to disregard the rules of international society, is considered irresponsible and damaging to international order.

Here the conventional democratic wisdom can be seen as clearly inadequate. Such voluntary standards of conduct did not prevent World War I or World War II. They did not prevent the enormities of Hitler's concentration camps and Stalin's gulag archipelago. They do not effectively protect standards of civilization elsewhere. The League and the UN Charter are particularly relevant. They were designed to provide universal and therefore, so to speak, legitimate machinery for enforcing international order. Their inadequacy – the gap between what they provide and the necessary minimum – can I think be summarized under two headings. First, they provide insufficient effective force unless that force is provided and when necessary delivered by a hegemonial power or group of powers. Second, they provide altogether insufficient machinery for orderly change.

However, *pacta sunt mutanda.* Times change, and contracts therefore need revision. It is easy enough to compile a long list of cases where the fulfilment of an alliance or a loan agreement has become more onerous than when it was contracted. Detailed arrangements may lose their relevance: for instance, NATO dispositions specifically designed to meet the Soviet threat. Also governments and electorates change their minds about what is acceptable. Today a whole range of international commitments like the law of the sea, which were freely entered into and indeed welcomed at the time, are being actively modified. In these cases responsible behaviour, in the Western view, involves adequate notice to the other parties, and an orderly revision of agreements by negotiation in which all parties have an obligation to show elasticity and willingness to compromise. Smaller and weaker governments do not reject these codes of conduct: they agree to observe them as a rule. But they insist that they must be allowed to make exceptions when observance would damage their interests, and that intervention to enforce contractual obligations is impermissible. More radical revisions, such as territorial boundaries, are still harder to achieve within the limits of conventional responsible behaviour.

Here we must remember that the contracts and standards of responsible behaviour are themselves conditioned by cultural assumptions. Independent political entities make agreements within a general framework, just as individuals and companies in a state make contracts within the framework of the law. Sometimes the international framework is purely regulatory, like the elaborate capitulations worked out between the Ottoman empire and European states. Any such framework of rules and institutions for managing the pressures of an international system could be called a society of states. Whereas capitulations are regulations shaped by mutual convenience, in much closer groupings whose members belong to the same culture and are at roughly the same stage of development (though not all necessarily independent) the rules, and particularly the codes of conduct, are shaped in a **cultural matrix**. One major reason why the European society of states was able to manage its affairs reasonably successfully for long periods is that it was culturally a single great republic. Insofar as membership of the same culture conditions the behaviour of political entities to one another, it transcends the freedom of action of those entities, and imposes significant though often uncodified limits on their independence. It seems to me what we call the present worldwide international society is in practice largely a highly developed set of regulatory capitulations, and that the additional limits imposed by a common culture also apply to some extent only because the major powers belong to or recognize an extended European culture, and are able to impose their views on others.

OBLIGATIONS TO HUMANITY AND THE ENVIRONMENT

The obligations of a state in the outer circle – to all humanity including the human rights discussed in the last chapter, and beyond that to other living things and the environment – are coming into increasing international prominence as the world shrinks. In contrast to the precise contracts of the second circle, they are still largely nebulous and unformulated. The specific current forms of obligation, especially those concerning weapons of mass destruction, drugs and the environment, are a recent innovation in the long history of relations between political entities, because they derive in large part from new problems created by man's increasing technological control over nature, and in particular by two consequences of technology, growing inter-involvement and the population explosion. The particular purposes of the obligations are very diverse. What they have in common is the sense that, while the obligations are couched in the form of contracts between sovereign and independent states, they deal with issues where in principle all states, and in practice particularly the rich and powerful and the highly developed ones, have responsibilities which transcend sovereignty.

The idea that rulers and governments have a moral obligation to individuals outside their own jurisdiction, and that non-governmental citizens and bodies such as churches also have such obligations, has a long history. A common form has been the obligation to spread the true religion; and since Islam for instance is a way of life rather than merely a creed, the diffusion of religion is bound up with the diffusion of culture. As God's truth gave way to self-evident truth, enlightened opinion has become more concerned with the abolition of slavery, the propagation of democracy, the elimination of disease, saving the rain forests and the whales. In their present form these aims largely reflect values of Western provenance, though perhaps of universal validity. Western democracies like to declare that we are all in some sense trustees for mankind and for the planet. But the obligations of this trusteeship remain for the most part unspecific, at best a *contrat tacite*.

In the present international climate, there are two ways to promote these aims. One is to codify some of these inchoate and tacit responsibilities, and so turn them into contractual obligations between states within the framework of multiple independences: in other words to move them into the second and more precise circle. Examples of this approach are the human rights clauses of the Helsinki Agreement, the nuclear non-proliferation agreements and the conventions on whaling. But on other pressing issues, like the cultural freedom of minorities in nation–states, atmospheric pollution, the tropical rain forests and the Arctic and Antarctic regions, the responsibilities of states have not yet been acceptably defined. Nor is any consensus on how to induce or ensure compliance yet visible on the horizon. The only effective way to promote such aims is by hegemonial pressure, using both carrots and sticks. And indeed it can be argued that the existing contractual agreements in these fields would not have been reached without a considerable amount of hegemonial inducement.

It is a real step forward to recognize the nature of the problem, and where responsibility lies. We saw in the last chapter that the powerful and developed states, particularly in the West, consider that they have an obligation to get their standards of civilization implemented outside their jurisdiction. It may seem that the responsibilities which the United States and like-minded governments accept in these fields are essentially restricted to the field of foreign policy, and to be implemented by the existing machinery of dealings between substantially independent states. Certainly these governments say, and intend, that this will continue to be their practice. But their economic, humanitarian and environmental demands already limit severely the local autonomy of many other states, and would if fully obeyed curtail them much further. Most of the global problems that concern the West are both intractable and urgent. The question arises: can they be dealt with adequately on a basis of voluntary compliance within the framework of multiple independences? Or are they problems not of international but of supranational order?

RESPONSIBILITY AND POWER

So we come back to the role of hegemonial authority. The current Western concept of international responsibility covers not only the obligations of independent states to their citizens, to each other and to the ecosystem. It also covers the questions of how far, and why, governments are willing, or obliged, to relinquish individual decision-making.

In the theory all the member states of our international society have the same external obligations, as all are held to be equal juridically. In practice some states are much more responsible for what happens internationally than others, simply because of their weight in the purely mechanical sense. Mechanical responsibility has some important practical consequences. For instance the members of the European international society, the 'sovereigns' club', came to treat each other as formal equals, but they accepted the special and obvious functional responsibilities of **great powers**. That was a loose collective form of the hegemony which is always present to some degree in systems of substantially independent states. The responsibility of the strongest power or powers for the functioning of the society increases as we move away from multiple independences towards dominion.

What is striking about the European society of states was not that voluntary restraint occasionally broke down into prolonged and horrendous warfare. It is more remarkable that it was able to function adequately for long periods on a basis of voluntary limits to the independence of its member states. Historians like Alfred Zimmern and Martin Wight have studied how far that society put the great powers under special obligations and restraints, both formal and tacit, 'encouraging their transformation from great powers to great responsibles'.[4] But in the European society of states there was no guarantee that the behaviour of great powers would always be what statesmen considered responsible. To be a great power is a matter of fact rather than status. During this century the four most effective generators of power, and those therefore with the greatest mechanical responsibility, have been the United States, Germany, Japan and Russia. The first half of the century saw irresponsibility reach the point of catastrophe twice. The irresponsibility was not confined to one or two powers, and the sins of omission were as great as the sins of commission.[5]

We in the West are culturally conditioned to think that all responsibility, and particularly hegemonial authority, involves both prudence and moral obligation. Prudence is the most responsible virtue of statesmanship.[6] It is the virtue which enables a statesman to bring practical and moral goals into some form of approximation with the stubborn and less than hospitable realities of international politics. The expediency of prudence shades off into the twin virtue of European statecraft, the sense of moral obligation. This ethical sense, unlike calculated prudence, has become stronger as the influence of public opinion on foreign policy grows.

Our international society is derived from the European, and therefore European practice and experience are especially relevant. Other systems, particularly in Asia, have had a corresponding ethical awareness. The teaching of Confucius is almost synonymous with moral responsibility. More recently countries of non-European origin have formulated, and gained general acceptance for, new ethical principles like racial equality and the need for collective economic aid, that are of great value in themselves and of great consequence for the functioning of international society. Such principles usually work to the direct benefit of those who advocate them, whereas the obligation falls on others who only benefit more indirectly. It would seem that in our society the concept of moral obligations which are not linked to material advantage is derived from Western theory and practice, and its ethical assumptions fit badly with some other cultures and political traditions.

DOES RESPONSIBILITY TRANSCEND INDEPENDENCE?

We can sum up the different aspects of international responsibility in today's world by noting that our second category, of contractual obligations of states to one another and to international bodies, and also most of our first category, the obligations of a democratic government to its electorate, fit comfortably into the framework of substantially independent states that is still the basic and cherished legitimacy of our society. However, reponsibilities of a state to mankind and to the environment reach beyond its jurisdiction, and so transcend independent statehood. The same can be said, indirectly, of the controversial and politically risky responsibility of a democratic government in our first category, to look beyond the momentary wishes of the majority of its electorate.

In the area which I see as the promotion of standards of civilized behaviour, ranging from commercial law and economic policy through arms and drug control to human rights and the environment, we are groping for a new conceptual framework as well as new techniques. Statesmen, professionals and academics increasingly recognize that results satisfactory to the West will not be achieved simply by voluntary consensus, and that a degree of hegemonial inducement is and will continue to be necessary. In fact a considerable amount of hegemonial pressure is already being applied in all these fields, especially by the United States which is in the best position to apply it. But given the legitimacy of sovereign statehood, and the great importance which newly independent states attach to it, it seems to most statesmen and observers very desirable that hegemonial pressure should be applied, or at least seem to be applied, as if between independent states.

Can such an approach produce enough results to satisfy Western opinion? So soon after wholesale decolonization, is it more likely to succeed, on balance, than a new and more naked approach? Is it more prudent to make use of the fig leaf of multilateral endorsement of what is really hegemonial action – a legitimation which the United Nations, the World Bank, the Nuclear Non-proliferation Treaty, the Universal Declaration on Human Rights and so on can provide?

There is obviously no general answer to this question. The rich donor states have the ability to make compliance with their standards a condition of meeting some of the economic needs of weaker states. Perhaps the minimum to establish in each particular case would be agreement or broad concurrence among the major powers to act in certain ways themselves, and then by collective hegemonial pressures (the carrot more often than the stick) to induce others to conform to their standards of civilization and ecological prudence. That can be done effectively while leaving the legitimacy of nominal sovereignties and a degree of domestic autonomy in place.

The difficulty with this approach is that international (as we still call it) practice is moving along the spectrum towards a more hegemonial authority, which increasingly prescribes the domestic behaviour of states. As it does so, it will find itself increasingly at variance with yesterday's legitimacy, the rules and institutions of our society. The strains which this disparity produces are destabilizing, though they do not unduly worry the hegemonial powers.

To recognize the realities of the situation is not just a matter of intellectual clarity. If problems that transcend sovereignty continue to grow in magnitude and urgency, we will want to consider more effective means of dealing with them. It seems to me that their solution may well require a supranational hegemonial authority in practice.

NOTES

1 Pierre Hassner, *International Affairs*, vol. 66, 3 July 1990.
2 The national interest of a state conventionally means what works to the net advantage of that state and its people. It is confusing to use it, as some recent writers have done, to mean what interests the public, or what the public wants its government to do.
3 One advantage for a democratic government in assuming hard contractual obligations to other states in the fields of economic and defence policy, as opposed to mere understandings, is that electorates accept a ratified treaty obligation more easily than a mere statement of their government's policy. This ensures greater continuity and predictability in international relations.
4 Martin Wight, *Systems of States*, Leicester University Press, 1977, p. 42.
5 It is worth noting that the compilers of the Anglican prayer book, following tradition, put 'We have left undone those things which we ought to have done' before 'we have done those things which we ought not to have done'. So also Thucydides makes the Corinthians, in their appeal to the Spartans to save them from Athenian aggression, say, 'The true author of the subjugation of a polis is not so much the immediate agent as the power which permits it when it could prevent it.'

6 One school of thought held that prudence was almost all that was required. If the members of an international society of independent states prudently and perceptively pursued their own interests, or *raison d'état*, and avoided ideological crusades, then the balance of power and international law would produce a quasi-automatic regulation of that society, like the unseen hand that regulates a market economy. But in practice statesmen were usually aware that they cannot count on the unseen hand, but must take active steps to make the system itself work. *Raison de système* means not a commitment to the status quo, but the management of orderly change. Maintaining a just balance between independent states requires continual ad*just*ment. Among the maxims that formulate the wisdom born of experience, none is more important than the rule that the enemy of today will be the ally of tomorrow, and that therefore you should not damage the vital (as opposed to the peripheral) interests of another state, especially a powerful state. Western traditions of statecraft are based on the prudence, the restraint, the elasticity, the sense of responsibility of a sophisticated elite, above the passions of the crowd. *Raison de système* is thus enlightened expediency, or farsighted prudence. The tragic lesson of the first half of this century is that such sophisticated voluntary restraints are not enough.

7 New perspectives on the states system

We have been examining various limits to independence. They include the familiar external curbs on the freedom of action of states that nevertheless remain in essence completely sovereign. But some limits go beyond that, and encroach on what used to be meant by independence. The walls which, in the European and the UN theory of sovereign statehood, separate independent states from each other are being breached.[1] The erosion has reached the point where it offers us new ways of looking at the pressures and interests that bind our states system closer together, and at the rules and practices with which we try to manage the tightening system. And we can also discern patterns in the relations between states which are not visible if we limit ourselves to independence. This is where the cutting edge of the theory of 'international' relations now seems to be.[2]

DEPENDENCE AND INDEPENDENCE

The words dependence and independence have meant different things at different times. But like many such expressions they retain echoes of their former meanings, and even assumptions that those meanings are still valid. These echoes may be politically and rhetorically useful, but they hinder clear understanding. Our present concept of sovereign independence for political entities is narrower than we sometimes suppose, and considerably more recent.

At the beginning of the European states system the Emperor Charles V alone was sovereign in the Habsburg dominions. His native Netherlands, his Austrian, Spanish, Greek and other domains were administered separately from each other: they were not dependencies of a core imperial state. But we should hesitate to call them independent in our sense. Soon after that, government in European states gradually and unevenly devolved from the ruler to the people, or more specifically the electorate. The shared sovereignty – the state – became more abstract, so that a king ceased to be the personification of the state, as the Emperor Charles and Louis XIV were, and became its first servant, as Frederick the Great was. The devolution of government at the centre was sometimes achieved by armed rebellion, but as often by negotiation and consent. However some territories under the new joint sovereignty, especially those outside Europe, did not participate in the devolution: the people or electorates of those territories might enjoy extensive local autonomy, but were excluded from the policy-forming process at the centre. Those territories became dependencies or colonies of a central or metropolitan state in a different and more modern sense. The words had changed their meaning.

The history of decolonization, from the 1770s to the present, is one of the gradual liquidation of political and administrative dependence on another state. It also took place in some cases by rebellion and in others by consent. Dependence was ended either by forming new, separate and wholly independent states, by the states in question becoming independent, or (more rarely) by absorbing the territories into the imperial state through an extension of citizenship and the franchise. Decolonization is thus the logical and conscious extension outside Europe of the devolution of sovereignty from the ruler to the electorate in the European *grande république*. In the course of this devolution a state like Canada or Australia can become independent in practice without being wholly so in constitutional theory.[3] And we have seen how common the converse is.

The achievement of independence used to be a simple and rather heroic affair. The classic and still inspiring example is the thirteen British colonies in North America which seceded to become the United States.[4] At that time independence meant self-reliance. It came at a price. There was fighting in both North and South America, and sometimes also economic loss.[5] The Europeans who achieved independence in Europe or the Americas did not ask for or expect economic support: either from the former imperial power, or from its enemies who may have helped them secede, or from the international society as a whole. The newly independent states accepted that they would have to stand on their own feet economically. The same was true strategically. The Atlantic Ocean was wide enough to allow the settler states in the Americas to avoid entangling alliances, but new states in Europe had to make alliances for their own protection like other states. Client allies expected subsidies, but in return for specific services.

In the heyday of wholesale decolonization after World War II the accepted meaning of dependence and independence changed again, as befitted the transition from a European to a global international society. The revolt against European domination, led by European-educated elites, created conditions of potential and occasionally actual disruption. It became clear to the European colonial powers that law and order could be more effectively maintained if the government of the dependent states was turned over to the elites. For this and other reasons described in Chapter 3, the European colonial powers were brought to the conclusion that most of the purposes for which they had established non-settler overseas dependencies could in future be as well or better achieved in a framework of nominal independence.

This was not independence in the former European and American sense of standing on one's own feet. Nor was it independence in conventional usage, which Webster's dictionary defines as 'Exemption from reliance on, or control by, others; self-subsistence or maintenance; direction of one's own affairs without interference'. Most of the newly independent states outside Asia would continue to need extensive economic, administrative and technical aid, including special marketing advantages for their principal products. But the decolonizers realized that sovereignty and administration could be transferred without all the attributes and capacities that had hitherto been considered their essential features. The concept of *collective strategic security,* formulated in the League Covenant and continued in the United Nations Charter, already made the society of states as a whole responsible for protecting its members from 'aggression'. The obligation was now extended to *collective economic security* where necessary – that is, where the newly independent governments wanted the aid and the donors were willing to give it. As Jackson says, the newly independent states are now in principle both guaranteed and paid for by international society.

Hobbes conceived the principal function of the Leviathan state to be the organized protection of its subjects, from foreign foes and from each other. But it does not follow that a state has to be politically independent to organize protection and order. The history of European colonization shows that the Europeans became involved in government outside Europe, and set up dependent states on the European model, in order to do just that. Now on the contrary our contemporary international society finds it expedient to treat as independent states many weak political entities that cannot organize protection and order for themselves. Formal independence is now a term of art, a legal status, not a description of a state's real or substantive functions.

The new meaning we have given to independence is thus very different from former ones. It does not exclude dependence, and is indeed designed to cover a substantial degree of it. Nor is it another term for colonialism. The present collective arrangements for small and weak states are a generalized substitute for individual colonial administration. They achieve most of the same purposes in new ways. In that sense they can be called neo-colonial; but the word is pejorative, and better left for polemics. The essential difference is that the aid, and the economic, political and social stipulations that go with the aid, are now operable only insofar as the new governments are willing to accept the package of conditions offered to them. Sometimes a recipient government will accept the donors' package only under considerable pressure and even duress involving military intervention. In most cases the new governments dislike the conditions, but they need the aid, and so they take it[6] and swallow the medicine.

Under the post-colonial dispensation the former imperial powers, the other donors and international society generally are able to obtain results comparable to the benefits to them of colonial administration, in return for less blood, less money, and less responsibility. Those who saw colonial rule as exploitation are still dissatisfied with the new dispensation, but less so. Those who considered it irresponsible of the colonizers to abandon the backward states before establishing more stable democracies and socially juster societies, can also console themselves that continuing pressure to achieve these aims is a central feature of the new arrangements. In practice, so far, new governments often conform less to Western standards of civilization than the former imperial regimes; and would conform even less but for pressure by the donors. As we saw in Chapter 5, many of the new states are still somewhat unused to democracy, and may need the 'surgical clamp' of firmer government than is now customary in developed Western countries.

THE DYNAMIC OF PRIVATE ENTERPRISE

This study of the limits of independence is primarily concerned with states, and the relations between them. But as we saw particularly in Chapter 3, the main element in the mix of motives that impelled the Europeans to bring the whole world into a single system was not politics but trade. The dynamic that pulled the world together was primarily economic, and moreover the dynamic of private enterprise.

From the beginning the motive force that drove the traders was to realize, so far as the circumstances of the time and place permitted, the potential of a completely free worldwide market.

The goal of worldwide free trade is now envisaged in the GATT negotiations and the World Trade Organization, but still from a distance: a global market place has not yet been realized, and its economic opportunities continue to open up. As opportunities expand, those enterprises thrive which make the most successful use of them. The global economy evolves in much the same way as, according to Darwin and Dawkins, in the world ecology those living organisms thrive which adapt themselves most successfully to changing circumstances.

What is the role of states in this scenario? In the main, the flags followed the trade. In the early stages private economic enterprises (including European settlements) were anchored to a single state, and usually operated by charter from that state. The enterprises looked to their state for protection: mainly from European competitors, and also but less from local threats. The Spanish and Portuguese governments provided some protection from the beginning; the Dutch, French and English governments preferred to leave the task and expense of providing security largely to their chartered companies. But all the governments in question derived increasing wealth and power from taxation of those enterprises and others that benefitted at one remove. Governments saw the advantage of using some of the money so derived to protect the geese that laid the golden eggs. European governments (including those of Russia and the United States) therefore undertook, or let themselves be dragged, usually with some reluctance, to make areas outside Europe safer for their settlers and traders, especially in the Americas.[7] Safety required not only military protection, but also the introduction of order into the dangerous free-for-all of European activities outside the *grande république*. Order involved inter-governmental agreements.

Thus the unruly dynamic of European competitive private enterprise led European governments to expand their individual authority, and also the practices of their international society, beyond the confines of the *grande république*. This did not happen all at once. For a long time the rules and codes of conduct which European states tried to impose outside Europe were looser and more purely expedient than in Europe itself. We can note four milestones on the road to our present global society, remembering that the stages were not reached simultaneously all round the world.

The safety of overseas commerce was the purpose of the earliest European attempts to expand their states system. The first regulatory steps towards that goal were agreements between governments. The capitulatory agreements made by European states with the Ottomans and the first European consulates in the Levant were designed to protect European merchants. The Spanish–Portuguese agreements to divide the overseas world into mutually exclusive hemispheres of operation aimed at the security of trade and (in the Americas) settlement.

A second stage in the expansion of the European states system was reached when individual European governments assumed the administrative responsibilities for non-European populations and territories which private companies had acquired to further their commerce and in some cases settlement, but which had become too much for a private enterprise. Each of the warring governments organized its own areas of protection and order by establishing dependent states on the European model. This was a gradual process: it was pioneered by Spain with its viceroys in the Americas, and reached its effective conclusion with the replacement of the British East India company by a government viceroy in 1858. At that stage each European state or company was still able to act much as it felt was expedient.

A third milestone in the creation of a worldwide order was reached in the nineteenth century, when the concert of European great powers was able to put an effective end to overseas conflicts between Europeans. Areas of collective responsibility for order and the protection of commerce were established by negotiation, most notably in China. Agreements between governments also delimited much greater areas of exclusive imperial government in dependent colonial states. The code of conduct observed by the expanding European states is illustrated by the exchanges between Gorchakov and Russell described in Chapter 3: the governments imposed the rules and codes of their society worldwide. In that phase too the orderly furtherance of private economic activity was the main, though not the only, motive for the actions of governments.

As the European states expanded their authority, they enforced the rules of their international society and also certain ethical and prudential restrictions on the single-minded quest for profit. Private companies lost some of their extra-European freedom of action and became increasingly regulated. But as state authority expanded, so too did the three restraints listed at the beginning of Chapter 1. The growing economic and strategic pressures of the international system, the extension of the rules of the international society, and the hegemonial European concert all constrained the actions of the powers and limited their independence of action outside the developed world.

In our own day economic factors made up a large, perhaps the largest, part in the mix of motives that brought European states to the most recent milestone of general decolonization. Most European settler states acquired independence or extensive autonomy before the twentieth century. But at least up till the Second World War, and sometimes afterwards, imperial governments considered that in non-settler territories it paid them and their entrepreneurs to maintain order by administering dependent states. After 1945 the growing insistence on political independence, by subject peoples and by the two superpowers, convinced other imperial governments that it would pay private enterprises and the imperial states themselves better on balance to turn over the administration of their dependencies to local elites.

Thus the originally European states system expanded geographically worldwide, and evolved into the international society of nominal multiple independences that we know today, largely as a result of economic dynamics and in the wake of commercial enterprise. In recent times the continuity of this long-term pattern was somewhat obscured. For most of the twentieth century it was plausible to think that the developed economies of the world were moving inexorably towards state ownership of the commanding heights of the economy, both in a state's territory and operating from its territory. The sectors of the economy open to innovation by private enterprise would continue to shrink, it was supposed, and what remained would be ever more regulated by the state. Marxist theory, the apparent permanence of the Soviet Union, and the spread of similar regimes made it seem that 'capitalism' would be superseded by forms of socialism or communism. Now it seems more plausible to think of the integration of the world into a single economy as the spinning of a vast web of private enterprise, with states becoming gradually involved in protecting and regulating it. Or the whole process, from the fur traders and the East India companies onwards, can be seen as the evolution of a global capitalism, not in the marxist sense of exploitation but rather as the most effective means of generating wealth by satisfying demand at both ends of the long trading runs. We noted in Chapter 1 that European economic enterprise was sucked into the rest of the world by the opportunities which opened up for it.

However, governments had and have other political purposes as well as the furtherance of private enterprise. With these other ends in view almost all governments today, from those that preside over immense concentrations of economic power like the United States and Japan down to the economically weakest clusters of islands, acknowledge the responsibility to pursue these other ends. Private enterprises operate so as to maximize their profits. Governments not only encourage and protect the operations of their private companies, but also regulate, channel and divert them. Such regulation aims to make entrepreneurs more responsible – that is, more ethical, more prudent, more peaceful, and above all to serve better the interest of the regulating state. Indeed some consider that the regulation of economic activity (rather than the extremes of ownership or *laisser faire*) is the most important function of governments in contemporary Western democracies. Many treaties, rules and codes of our international society are designed to further the same aims. These intergovernmental understandings bring into the realm of practical politics curbs on private enterprise which individual governments are unwilling to apply unilaterally.

In the present phase of economic liberalization and freer trade, state control of economic life has relaxed and private enterprises have recovered some of their ability to conduct their operations in the most profitable way. As they do so, they become more global and less centred in a particular state. Some long-range enterprises come close to detaching themselves from any state, and become pipelines connecting sources of production and consumption round the world, uniting supply to demand as the classical economists put it. Not only great 'multinational' corporations (the term is misleading), but many small companies still centred in one state are becoming more responsive to the dynamism of a world economy, and move some of their activities out of the state in which they are incorporated to more profitable areas like the Caribbean, Eastern Europe and China. At the same time various aspects of aid and development that used to be conducted largely by state agencies are now being privatized and 'marketized', and multilateral aid organizations like the World Bank and the IMF foster private rather than state enterprises in Africa, the former Soviet Union and elsewhere. Privatization lightens the burden on the taxpayers of developed countries and relieves donor fatigue, and it adapts the development of dependent states more closely to the dynamic of private enterprise that has brought about the integration of the world.

A useful illustration is provided by the world capital market. Most governments, including notably the United States, as well as private companies that operate across state borders, borrow money internationally. State and interstate agreements can influence the rates at which they can do this to some extent, but the rates are determined by what lenders consider the appropriate balance between risk and reward. The rates of exchange of convertible currencies are determined in the same way. Money has again become global and largely independent of governments, as it was when based on gold.

All this is a significant change from earlier practice. The individual Leviathan state seems less of an all-devouring whale or boa-constrictor than capitalists feared. It is now possible to talk of liberalization hollowing out states and the multilateral agencies that act for states, until they are only shells.

One must not push these metaphors beyond the realities they are designed to illustrate. Liberalization in the developed Western democracies is a policy of states, pursued with the consent of the majority of the electorate. It is the hegemonial concert of economic powers that causes the multilateral government agencies to encourage and act through private enterprise. The recipient states deregulate and liberalize their economies in response to the carrots and sticks of the donor states, though some recipient governments are themselves convinced that liberalization will bring them economic benefits. Beyond the actions of individual governments, the whole global economic regime in which our international society functions is established and managed by states. Intergovernmental conventions formulate stricter ethical and environmental standards than before. Commercial enterprises are on the whole more aware of them than they were in the past, and more inclined to conform to them, though numerous scandals show that reputable companies and governments (not to mention the illegal drug and arms mafias) still occasionally flout both international agreements and Western ethical standards in the quest for profit. Certainly the independence of states is now being limited in many ways. The world may be moving towards a greater supranational authority, or a number of such authorities, formed by a mixture of hegemonial pressure and voluntary agreement. Supranational communities, unions or leagues tend to limit their member states increasingly to local autonomy, and enable economic activity to operate more according to its own logic within the limits set by supranational controls. But at present states, and the international society of states, are still much more than shells. How long this phase will last it is impossible to say.

THE RECIPIENT–DONOR LIST

We saw in Chapter 4 how diverse and unlike each other states and political entities are. One important difference is that they function differently in the system. The role of the strongest states in ensuring the strategic security of the smaller and weaker ones, and of the system as a whole, is obvious. The threat of international conflict is real, especially in certain restless areas like the Middle East. But most states, and particularly the less rich ones, are more concerned with economic than strategic security, more anxious about prosperity than international peace. How do states function differently in the present phase, as their economies are increasingly involved in the worldwide web of private enterprise and technology?

Let us list the states in our present system in order of their dependence. The list begins with those who need the largest proportion of outside assistance and would be least able to manage alone. It continues through states ever more able to stand on their own feet, until we reach states or areas which help to provide assistance to others, and ends with hegemonial and imperial powers that radiate their aid, influence and authority through part or all of the system. The donors consist of individual donor states acting in their own name, notably Japan, the United States and some West European and Arab countries; international institutions like the World Bank and the Monetary Fund that act on their behalf; and non-governmental institutions ranging from banks to charities. Let us call this list the recipient–donor list. The way the member states function in the system, i.e., how they are constrained by its pressures to act, and also how they consciously decide to act as members of the international society, will depend to a large extent on their position on our list. In other words, how they function externally is, to a large degree but not entirely, a factor of their dependence.

An imperial system, or more exactly subsystem, may be said to exist where client ministates derive their technical and economic aid from a single major power. In such circumstances the imperial power usually also provides a measure of political underpinning or enforcement of minimum standards, and a proportion of the intellectual elite in the ministates look to the imperial power for their higher education and some of their values.

The amounts of aid are impressively large. They are not as large as the recipients would like, and they may be reduced by donor fatigue, the growing and visible reluctance of donor democracies to spend so much on aid. Figures also vary according to what is counted (for instance the salaries of French school teachers seconded to Africa) and rates of exchange. As examples, the Japanese government spends about $11 billion a year (£7,000 million) on official aid programmes, the US government nearly as much. Private US foundations, religious and other charities give about 20 per cent more than their government. At the other end of the aid pattern, I have not seen any convincing way of reckoning the benefits which dependent countries derive from the sugar and other quotas accorded by the European Union and the United States, compared to what those countries would get for the same products in a free market.

Certainly the various forms of aid, taken together, materially help to integrate the world's economies, just as European imperialism did, and they increasingly involve the donors as well as the recipients in the responsibility for standards of civilization.

The conventional image of the donor–recipient relationship is that it is a temporary one. In it dependent recipients, most of them nevertheless slowly emerging into independence, confront independent donor powers that can unilaterally regulate the direction and extent of their aid according to the democratic pressures of their electorates and the circumstances of their economy. That is only part of the picture. The donor powers too are involved – one might say enmeshed – in a symbiosis with the recipients on the one hand and with their partners in the joint economic hegemony on the other. The various forms which aid now takes include production of goods and services which utilize otherwise unused capacity in the donor economies, and protected markets for the goods produced by donors as well as recipients. Taken together they amount to much more than merely a commitment that the donors might find it diplomatically and strategically awkward to break. They establish patterns of mutual involvement that affect jobs, prices, infrastructure and ultimately votes in both donor and recipient countries.

Economic activity is like a river: the water seeks to find its own level. All successful political influence on economic activity inevitably diverts, and is intended to divert, the flow of that activity. Colonialism obviously did so. Multilateral aid to developing countries, including privileged markets for certain of their products, does so too. The patterns of mutual involvement created by aid are likely to prove more durable than is often supposed.

The standards of civilization set by the donors also form part of the complex equation. The internal structure of states with a high degree of dependence is conditioned by the need to meet the requirements imposed by the donors. Of course the donors are not always unanimous: aid and support are available from different sources. During the cold war several states switched their dependence from one side to the other; and modified their internal structure and forms of government accordingly.[8] In the present phase, the donors are predominantly Western and democratic; there is not much alternative for recipient states other than to conform or partially conform to various Western values as conditions of aid. How long the current phase will last is uncertain. We saw that as powerful Asian states reassert themselves, the values demanded by donors may alter.

It is misleading to limit the term dependence to dependence on a single power. The desire of dependent states to spread their dependence, to deal with international institutions and to benefit from economic and strategic collective security, preserves the forms of sovereign independence and something of the substance. The donor powers too prefer to act through the legitimacy of international institutions: not just for the figleaf of respectability, which often does not hide very much, but also because legitimacy is the lubricating oil of an international society, and because the donors want to spread their responsibility just as the recipients want to spread their dependence.

It seems to me therefore that increasing involvement is moving our international society of states along the spectrum away from the anarchical extreme of multiple independences towards a more hegemonial authority. The formerly dependent states are emerging not into real independence in its former sense but into a more integrated system, which is usually described by that overworked word interdependence. As the net tightens, integration is bound to erode sovereignty, and to reduce the independence of the smaller and weaker states to a small core of jurisdiction that could be called sovereign autonomy. This core will presumably include the trappings of sovereignty such as the flag and the seat at the UN. It will also include domestic administration within the limits set by donor conditions; the conditions may allow for a firmer executive and a greater degree of state authority than prevails in the donor states. And perhaps most importantly, both for the smooth working of the more hegemonial society and for the self-respect of the recipient states, sovereign autonomy needs to include the right to refuse aid when the recipient government finds the conditions unacceptable (the ability to do so in practice is another matter).

An interesting feature of the recipient–donor list is that if (as seems likely) the world continues to become more economically integrated and more interdependent, so that the sovereignty and independence of all states becomes more limited, even so the order of the political entities on the list is likely to change only gradually. The list thus provides a realistic, durable and perhaps most useful point of view from which to look at the relations between political entities in our current post-colonial system. It also has theoretical implications for the study of hegemony.

STATES AND SYSTEMS OF STATES

The present phase of relations between states, characterized by considerable hegemony and reflected in the recipient–donor list, has its place on the basic spectrum of relations between political entities. That place is somewhat further from the independences end than for instance the anarchical society of states described by Hedley Bull. Let us look at the pattern of our spectrum again as we keep these two examples in mind along with the others discussed in earlier chapters. Let us also consider the resemblance between a single political entity and a complex system of such entities.

One function of a constituted state, whether sovereign or dependent, is to focus and give order to the relations between its individual and corporate members or citizens. The theoretical independence endpoint of the spectrum of relations between political entities supposes an absolute anarchy of multiple independences – a total absence of overarching order where every state would *ex hypothesi* be so independent that there would be no system, let alone an international society. There would be no possible analogy to a constituted state. As we move along the spectrum from the theoretical absolute into the realm of practice, we come first to limited degrees of involvement between neighbours, managed by local understandings. As the involvement increases, the understandings become formulated in capitulatory regulations like those between the Ottoman empire and the European grande république, and other similar arrangements. Further along the spectrum we find international societies – societies that are still anarchical, with no overarching authority, but whose member states manage their closer involvement with each other by consciously putting in place and when necessary modifying a set of rules, institutions and codes of conduct. So far as we can see, such societies always originate within the matrix of a dominant culture, and they are always characterized by a degree of hegemony. Some of them manage the delicate balance of independences remarkably well. Already at this stage we can say that even if the member states of such a society were born free,[9] in the sense that they were at some earlier stage genuinely sovereign and independent of each other, by now they are (to use

Rousseau's metaphor) everywhere in the chains of a social contract. The principal chains limiting their independence are the three kinds of restraint described at the beginning of Chapter 1: the impersonal pressures caused by involvement in a system; the rules and codes – the contract – of the society; and the hegemonial authority of the greatest powers. In this part of the spectrum an international society begins to correspond in a shadowy way to an individual state, insofar as it focuses and gives order to the conduct of its members.

The state-like focus and order become stronger as we move along the spectrum. One powerful state or a concert of powerful states exercises increasing hegemonial authority over the others, by some mixture of coercion and consent. In the process all the states in the system become more involved with each other; the restrictions on their freedom of action – the chains – become tighter. This is the area of the present phase, of the recipient–donor list. Further along our simplified diagram lies an area of suzerainty, where the smaller and weaker political entities formally or tacitly recognize the overlordship of an imperial power or concert. The inducements which make suzerainty acceptable in a whole system, together with additional local economic and security advantages, may lead some similar states to join in a voluntary and federal union. This is gradually happening in Europe today. I know no example of a substantially voluntary federation of a whole system of states.

In this middle section of the diagram a central authority controls not only the external relations of the member entities but some of their internal jurisdiction too, while leaving them a substantial degree of autonomous statehood. In practice there is some overlap: a hegemonial authority that does not have the status of a suzerain can still exert considerable influence over the internal affairs of lesser political entities, even though the legitimacy accords them the formal status of independent states. That was the position in the heyday of the Concert of Europe (the Metternich age, 1815–1848, described in Chapter 2), and it is the position in the present phase of Western hegemony described in Chapters 4 and 5. Already at this stage the distinction between a state's external relations and its domestic affairs is becoming blurred. What remains of the distinction diminishes as we move further along the diagram.

When we move beyond suzerainty we come to the area of the diagram I call dominion. The term must not be taken to imply a high degree of coercion. The middle ranges of the spectrum also cover voluntary associations, communities and federations. We have seen that both in Europe and in the relations between donor and recipient states the inducements to accept a greater degree of central authority are increasingly positive. There is currently a shift towards more voluntarism and less coercion, which is welcome to most people in the West as well as in former dependencies. In any case, when we reach this area of the spectrum we have moved from international to supranational systems. The states involved are no longer nominally independent: they are in practice provinces subordinate to a central government. As we continue through the area of dominion the autonomy of the states steadily diminishes and the overarching authority becomes more centralized and more monopolistic.

Then we move beyond dominion into that part of the diagram I have called empire. In it a very considerable concentration of central authority extends its control over a number of subordinate political entities that are still distinguishable but whose local autonomy is so diminished and subordinated that we can hardly still call them states. The system itself becomes steadily more like a single state. In the historical examples that we know of, the central authority operates with varying combinations of coercion and consent, from empires based almost entirely on military force, like that of Genghis Khan, to voluntary federations like the United States whose member states agreed to cede a great deal of power to a central authority which they or their citizens jointly elect. The range of compromises between coercion and consent in the imperial area of the spectrum is well illustrated in the European options discussed in Chapter 2. There we find three examples of highly concentrated authority: the centralized and coercive Nazi rule, the diffused coercion and consent of the Napoleonic empire, and the prospect (not yet the reality) of a European Union with a voluntary but increasingly powerful central overarching authority and diminishing local autonomy. A difficulty with the word empire for this part of the spectrum is that it suggests coercion, even if used in a technical or algebraic sense to mean any highly centralized system. Some scholars therefore prefer to use the milder term hierarchy.

The theoretical endpoint of total centralization (extrapolating ourselves from reality again) would be a single absolutely centralized universal imperial state, in which all distinctions between administrative entities would disappear. It can be seen as the point of infinity where the converging domestic and interstate lines would meet.

The relevance of this pattern becomes clearer if we now move back along the spectrum in the opposite direction. We would go from absolute centralization first to the point where distinct political entities are just discernible. We would then move on to the area of dominion, along which imperial or supranational authority becomes looser, and where local autonomies increase until they cease to be provinces and become separate but still partially dependent states. The pressures and restraints on the states lessen as we continue along the spectrum, until we reach the present decolonized international phase, where almost all political entities are recognized as independent states though many are still in fact dependent, and the whole international society is managed by a hegemony (in the present phase a collective Western hegemony, but in some other analogous cases that of a single power). The hegemony diminishes as we move further along; as we approach the theoretical independence endpoint of the spectrum, international society and even regulatory arrangements between states cease to operate, the impersonal pressures of the states system weaken to nothingness, all overarching authority and limits to independence disappear, and the states finally emerge into the full anarchy of multiple absolute independences.

The anarchophile idealization of independence and the nationalist aim to break up multinational states have led many to suppose that the further along the spectrum towards multiple independences the states system can be pushed, the greater will be the liberty not only of states but also of individuals. The assumption is unjustified. Clearly the goals of sovereignty (by definition) and nationalism do benefit by movement towards the multiple independences end. Those goals seemed desirable enough a hundred years ago. The lessons of two great wars have destroyed their appeal for most Westerners, but not for many others elsewhere. However there is no evidence that, in the broad area of the spectrum ranging from suzerainty to substantial independence in which the present phase is situated, the goals of peace and order, of material prosperity, and human rights are consistently furthered by movement one way or the other along the scale. The end of colonial rule pushed the international system a considerable way towards unlimited independences, and brought significant benefits to many. Equally welcome benefits to individuals have resulted from the movement back to greater hegemonic authority which has taken place since. The evidence is that hegemonic pressure and where necessary intervention have done much to promote peace, prosperity and especially the rights of individuals, in newly independent ex-colonies and in other ill-governed states like Haiti. Historical examples going back a long way into the past show that increasing the number of independent states does not necessarily mean greater happiness for a greater number of individuals.[10]

An interesting feature of this pattern is that a spectrum between anarchy and centralization of power also describes internal structures of individual states. Domestic government at its weakest is close to the theoretical absolute of anarchy where there is no state at all (Hobbes's nasty brutish and short existence). The state becomes tighter through increasing degrees of governmental authority and capacity for enforcement, and increasing curbs on the ability of the citizens to behave as they like. The actual balance of coercion and consent, and the degree of federal or unitary government, will vary from one example to another. The other end of the spectrum is the equally theoretical absolute of monolithic centralized power. A wholly centralized authority would not necessarily be a totalitarian 'Orwell plus' state that dictatorially controls every aspect of its subjects' lives: a totally centralized state could be a democracy.[11]

Thus the same diagram illustrates the range of both the internal organization or structure of a single political entity and the structure of a system of such political entities. At the theoretical endpoint of centralization, the total concentration of power in a system of states would turn what was a system into a single wholly centralized state. The diagram can be described as a zero-infinity range of order. Or it can be called an anarchy–hierarchy spectrum. However a difficulty with the term hierarchy is that as we extrapolate our diagram beyond reality and approach the theoretical absolute of an undifferentiated universal state, hierarchical gradations would decline to nothing.

Even so there is this essential difference, that a state or political entity in our sense is part of a whole that to some extent affects its conduct, whereas a system is that whole of which the states are a part[12] (ignoring the sporadic contacts of states and individuals outside their systems).

A third relevant aspect of the same spectrum can be seen in imperial structures of authority. As I have explained elewhere,[13] historical 'empires' (for instance that of Napoleon described in Chapter 2) radiate from a directly administered core through areas of dominion and local autonomy to more loosely controlled areas of hegemony; beyond the empire lie areas independent of its authority, with which it is in an anarchical relationship. The imperial pattern from hierarchy to anarchy applies today particularly, as we saw in Chapter 4, to aid, economic penetration and influence, rather than to military coercion.

THE PENDULUM

At several places in this book, and particularly in Chapters 2 and 3, we have noted movement along the spectrum. Pressures in the system – the extent to which states in it are involved with one another – are sometimes greater and sometimes less. We saw that the eighteenth-century independence of most of the settler colonies in the Americas loosened relations across the Atlantic; that in the following century European imperialism tightened the net round the states of the eastern hemisphere, and so moved the whole system away from anarchy towards hegemony; and that in the twentieth century new technology continued to tighten the net. All through the twentieth century the rules of international society have inclined towards anarchy and rejected effective curbs on independence, especially in the period of decolonization; but the impersonal pressures of technology have been imposing stricter practical limits on the independence of member states, and pushing the system towards ever greater hege-monial authority. In the last decades, after the heady years of decolon-ization, the system has in fact moved back from anarchic independence. The pendulum is an apt analogy for this to and fro movement. Each swing builds up a tendency to swing back the other way. The swings take place over a considerable period of time, so that the movement in one direction seems more permanent than it really is.

The four ways of looking at relations between political entities dis-cussed in this chapter can be summarized as follows. First, a state can be, and many states now are, juridically independent and highly dependent at the same time. Second, a recipient–donor list, which arranges states according to the degree of their dependence, is a real-istic way of indicating their relations. It records about half of them as *de facto* dependent – roughly the same half as were formally dependent before the last great decolonization. Third, the range between multiple independences and monolithic central authority along which we find systems of states – the range of increasing curbs on the freedom of action of states which we called the anarchy–hierarchy or zero-infinity control spectrum – corresponds to the same range between anarchy and control within individual states. And fourth, the pendulum is a useful analogy for the movement of systems and individual states in both directions along the spectrum: towards greater or lesser indepen-dence, towards more or less order. All four focus our attention on limits to the freedom of action of states, from the most weak and dependent to the hegemonial great powers.

The angles of vision described in this chapter are relevant to the evolving theory of the states system. But for them to clarify our understanding, we need to emancipate ourselves from what Martin Wight called 'the intellectual prejudice imposed by the sovereign state'. We must give up the anarchophile assumption that relations between independent states are now the only ones worth studying. In the heyday of decolonization hegemony was regarded as anachronistic and in the modern world disreputable. 'Lingering dependence' was to be overcome as quickly as practicable. We are now learning to look at hegemony, both individual and collective, as a relationship that is always present to some degree in even the loosest systems of states. We are more willing to examine its effects objectively, and to recognize that it brings some benefits, including the limits it imposes on independence.

NOTES

1 See Michael Fowler and Julie Bunck, *Law, Power and the Sovereign State*, Penn State University Press, 1995.

2 See especially the illuminating summary of present theoretical positions by Professors Buzan and Little, 'Reconceptualizing Anarchy' in the *European Journal of International Relations*, vol. 2/4, December 1996.

3 By the beginning of this century the dependence of British dominions like Canada and Australia had become transparently thin. The citizens of Perth, Australia could reasonably claim to be more self-governing than those of Perth, Scotland, because Western Australia enjoyed a provincial autonomy that Scotland did not; but at a stratospheric level the parliament at Westminster, which the electors of Perth, Scotland, helped to choose, had more imperial authority than the parliament at Canberra. The point is arcane in practice; but it is perhaps significant for a theory of dependence.

4 Elsewhere freedom did not necessarily mean independence from a remote or alien power. In the nineteenth century many, perhaps most, Italians and Germans felt that by joining together in a national state they were freeing themselves from the web of petty sovereignties that held them down, and achieving a new national independence. Similarly many or most Muslims in the Indian sub-continent in the 1940s wanted to free themselves from Hindu domination by joining together in a separate Pakistan.

5 De Valera told Herbert Butterfield that most peoples who wanted to be free were willing to pay an economic price, and that a majority of the Irish would accept a fall in their standard of living of about 12 per cent as the price of independence. The statistic was a joke, but the concept of a people willing to pay an economic price for freedom was not.

6 When Frederick the Great was told that the Empress Maria Theresa wept when accepting her share of Poland in the first partition, he is reported to

have said '*Elle a pleuré mais elle a pris*'. Today the governments of highly dependent states *pleurent, mais ils prennent.*

7 Governmental involvement was gradual, and the details are complex. In general, in the eighteenth century the British and French governments assumed direct responsibility for protecting their settlements in the Americas, and attacking the settlements of their rivals. Washington, Wolfe, Montcalm and their fellows commanded British or French governmental, not company, armies. But their contemporaries in India – Clive, Dupleix, Wellington – were agents of the companies. By the nineteenth century the imperial European states wished, and felt they could afford, steadily to assert more direct authority in Asia, and later in Africa. The purposes and responsibilities of imperial governments went beyond what could be expected from private enterprises operating for profit.

8 When Cuba, for instance, moved out of the United States imperium into the Soviet one, its dependence was not lessened: it received rather less material assistance, but obtained the military protection which it had not thought necessary when in the American imperium, as well as adopting a quasi-Soviet form of government.

9 To translate the first words of Rousseau's Contrat Social, '*L'homme est né libre*' as man *is* born free is due to ignorance of French.

10 Ira Straus puts it like this: 'The glorification of independence . . . has led people all round the world into thinking that they could fight for human rights simply by fighting for some new separation. Countless tragedies have resulted' (*International Herald Tribune*, 4 July 1995).

11 An element of coercion is apparently always present in democratic central authorities. Even so mild and determinedly democratic an overarching federal authority as that established by the United States Constitution developed strong coercive tendencies. The desire of the Southern states to secede was suppressed with ruthless force, though the proportion of their electorates (and indeed of their total populations) wishing to secede from Washington exceeded that which had favoured secession from Britain.

12 A familiar caveat of elementary international theory is the fallacy of the 'domestic analogy': treating a society of independent states as if it were like a society of individuals and corporations in a single state. There is an analogy between a state and a states system, as we have seen. But we can reasonably compare a state with a system only when they are at roughly the same position along the spectrum. In the light of our diagram, the fallacy of the domestic analogy can be seen as the error of comparing the essentially anarchic international society of sovereign or semi-sovereign states that we have today, or had yesterday, at a position well towards the multiple independences end of the diagram, with the domestic arrangements of a modern constituted state that possesses judiciary, police, tax collection and other resources of consent and enforcement, and is therefore much further towards the hierarchy and order end of the spectrum.

13 Adam Watson, *The Evolution of International Society*, Routledge 1992. See also Ole Waever, 'Europe's Three Empires. A Watsonian Interpretation of Post-War European Security', forthcoming in *Beyond International Society*, Faun, Larkins and Newman (eds), which contains diagrams of the imperial spectrum and the pendulum.

8 The contemporary practice of hegemony

It remains to see what practical advice we can distil from the evidence in the foregoing chapters, and from a clearer understanding of how our society of states functions. How does the present degree of collective hegemony affect these ends? How might we move the conduct of the day to day relations between states, and international society generally, in a direction that will be welcome to us? In looking for suggestions I will assume that anarchy, or inadequate limits to independence, is undesirable but all too likely, and that a single democratically chosen world government is so out of the present range of possibilities that its desirability is irrelevant to our question. How can we move the world as it is now, between the undesirable and the impossible, towards the mundane advantages of peace and order and greater material well-being?

HEGEMONIAL AUTHORITY

Perhaps the first step is to recognize the degree of hegemonial authority which now exists, and which the great powers exercise in practice. What we see is a loose informal concert of the strongest powers, with varying active membership and the United States as its outstandingly powerful member. Different groups of non-hegemonial states are consulted on various issues, as seems appropriate to those concert powers actively involved. The authority of this loose concert is not absolute, and not always successful, but the concert is effective enough to play a major part in world affairs. The concert inevitably leaves unresolved some of the problems it would like to resolve, or fails to solve them well. Such failures occur either because the circle cannot be squared and a solution is inherently too difficult to achieve, or because the members of the concert do not agree about what should be done.

In systems near the multiple independences end of the spectrum, especially those regulated by capitulatory conventions, expediency and the interests of the independent states are what matter, and differences of values scarcely affect international relations.[1] But we have seen that hegemonial authority is concerned not only with material advantages but also with standards of civilization.

Hegemonial pressure and inducements are not exercised at random. There is a perceptible general direction towards which they tend. Today's concert has three connected strands or categories of aim. All three restrain and limit the independence of other states.

The first is **peace** between states. The concert aims to undo military conquest, and to discourage future attempts. The periodic use of hegemonial force, for instance in the Gulf War and in Bosnia, should be seen as efforts to promote peace.

The second and most general aim is to promote economic well being and **prosperity**. The economic authorities of today's hegemonial powers see prosperity not as a mercantilist or zero sum game, but as bringing mutual benefits (including of course benefits to the donors and lenders). The concert usually operates in favour of economic liberalization, flexibility and interpenetration, and of strict, 'responsible' domestic economic policies, all of which impose curbs on the internal independence of states. But it prefers to leave the territorial jurisdictions of states as they happen to be.

Third, the Western members of the concert, and especially the United States, are also determined to support current (Western) **standards of civilization**: what are sometimes broadly described as missionary aims. This category of aims includes democracy; both kinds of human rights; and the protection of the environment. Not all, but most, of these purposes are familiar component elements of the standards of civilization which concerts of hegemonial powers have sought to promote for most of the last two centuries.

There is thus a long-term continuity in the general direction of hegemonial pressure. But the evidence shows that the authority and the effectiveness of the concert have varied greatly in the course of the last two centuries, and will doubtless continue to fluctuate. Also the emphasis changes on particular issues. In the first half of this century there was no real concert. After the Second World War, the cold war paralysed an effective concert on most issues. But even then there was sustained pressure on certain issues by both the United States and Soviet governments, as well as by public opinion in developed countries generally. The most important example was the pressure to end colonial administration by individual powers – to abolish dependent states as private preserves, so to speak.

Decolonization gave greater legitimacy to multiple independences and to sovereignty in the Third World just when the disadvantages of the anarchic end of the spectrum were becoming increasingly visible in other contexts. However in the longer perspective we saw in Chapter 3 that the individual empires had been largely established in the nineteenth century with the tacit approval of the concert, because they were held to promote order, economic development and standards of civilization. Now that they have been dissolved, the hegemonial powers see a need, or in more neutral language find it desirable, to limit both the external and the internal sovereignty of the formerly dependent states, and especially the newly independent and less viable ones, in order to promote what they now consider civilized standards of economic development, political governanace, human rights and the environment. Of course the hegemonial powers act in their own interest and according to their own principles. But in the present phase they have enough *raison de système* and sense of responsibility to see the general welfare of mankind as including benefits to themselves.

Our understanding of hegemonial authority requires us not merely to perceive the major part which it plays, but also to recognize that at present there is no other significant motive force in favour of the aims of peace and order, material well being, or protection of human rights and the environment. Diplomats used to mutter to each other that *tout s'arrange, mais mal*. Mal perhaps, but without the concert things would be much worse. What would happen if the strongest powers repudiated their hegemonial responsibilities? Let us suppose that some colossal upsurge of donor fatigue and moral indifference somehow removed all hegemonial pressures, inducements and aid from the international scene. Few if any will doubt that as one result economic prosperity, human rights, the protection of the environment and even military security would decline in the world. We should find ourselves in a world of states with less economic integration and fewer limits to their independence, working out a greater variety of individual cultural, political and economic approaches to their problems. Life would become less homogenized, more varied and more experimental, but as Hobbes warned, nastier and shorter.

We need not worry. In the present phase of international society the hegemonial authority of the great powers is not decreasing, but growing stronger and more pervasive. Even so the risk is not that they will do too much, but rather that they will do too little.

CHANGING STANDARDS OF CIVILIZATION

In earlier chapters we looked at intervention by the powers that directed the Concert of Europe to enforce what they deemed to be standards of civilization, beginning with the suppression of the Atlantic slave trade, in which Britain took the naval lead. We saw that most of those ventures were not collective enterprises, but were carried out by individual great powers: with an agreement, or sometimes no more than an acquiescence after protest, by the others about where and how each should operate. But there were also collective operations. The most prolonged and significant was the relationship with China. That immense collective undertaking took the form of a series of 'unequal' treaties and enforcements, involving principles such as the 'open door' for trade, and administrative arrangements like the international government of Shanghai; it reached its climax in the grand joint military intervention of 1900. In the century since then, Western standards of civilization have altered, but not very much.

We need to keep in mind that the standards of civilization we have been discussing in this book are in fact Western standards, formed within the matrix of European culture. Even values like the ideal of unfettered independence, which have now come to seem anarchical and dangerous to most Europeans, were developed in Europe and taught by Westerners to the rest of the world. The collapse of the Soviet Union and the end of the cold war, together with the continuing technological superiority of the West and especially the United States, have ushered in a phase of international society where all the great powers are prepared to accept or acquiesce in Western leadership, though sometimes very reluctantly. At present the donors are largely Western; and it is the Western states that exercise the negative or coercive inducements too. Consequently not only the material advances but also the standards of civilization, human rights and the environment promoted by the hegemonial concert are substantially Western.

The present phase is likely to be temporary. How long it will last is hard to foresee. Technology is proving to be by and large more culturally neutral than some people feared, and can be transposed fairly easily from one developed culture to another.[2] But most values and ethical judgements are not culturally neutral, in spite of the frequent assertion that they are. A potential future world concert will be confronted with a problem which the present Western-dominated concert does not face. The faster growth of the economic power and capacities of the great Asian states – in the first rank Japan, China, India and perhaps Indonesia – will ensure that their un-Western traditions and views carry increasing weight in the counsels of any world concert that may develop in the early years of the next century. A comprehensive concert with substantial Asian membership raises the cultural issue in more acute form than for some time. If a multicultural concert does develop, the values and aims which underlie its actions, and the standards of civilization by which it measures the actions of other states, will surely become less specifically Western.

The governments and more especially the publics of the United States and Europe must therefore get used to the idea of a medium- and long-range partnership with other major powers that do not exactly share our values. It will have to be a partnership that goes beyond acquiescence, perhaps to different leadership in various regions. There will need to be a broad agreement about the nature of international society and the use of hegemonial authority in it, and about the consultation and joint action necessary to manage inevitable change.

One likely modification is that the limits imposed by the donors on the internal independence of recipient states will probably become less strict. Another prospect is that the assistance given to the smaller and weaker states will enable them to stand more on their own feet, and that the dependence discussed in Chapter 4 will decline.

CHANGING IDEAS OF SOVEREIGNTY

The second major reality that we need to recognize is the change in the concepts of sovereignty and independence. The change is one consequence of the growth of hegemonial authority.

Interventionist pressure has reached the point where the majority of the concert powers, and Western opinion generally, no longer accept the basic premise of sovereignty, that the established government of any duly constituted and recognized state has a right to behave as it sees fit, without interference from other rulers. Internal sovereignty accorded to a recognized government of an independent state the right to maintain itself in power as it judged best, and to invite friendly external help in doing so. External sovereignty gave a recognized government the right to declare war in due form and to try to coerce another state. Due form was a procedural matter, bringing into operation the laws of war. The provisions of the League Covenant and the United Nations Charter extended the requirement to include the assent of the appropriate international organization. For example the Argentine government was unable to obtain that assent when it tried to 're-establish its sovereignty' by force over the Falkland Islands, and so was the Iraqi government when it tried to 're-establish its sovereignty' over Kuwait.

The rights of sovereigns were fairly generally respected by the related members of the European princes' club during certain periods; but they were also widely disregarded even then. Conspicuous examples are the French intervention under Lafayette in the secession of the British North American colonies, and the corresponding British aid to the rebels in the Spanish American colonies. The sovereigns of Europe regarded the interventions of the French revolutionaries in their internal affairs in the name of 'liberty' as illegitimate: but the cumulative effect of the revolutionary and Napoleonic wars was to make the sovereignty of European states less sacrosanct. From that time on, states have repeatedly intervened in each other's internal affairs. The repeated foreign interference in the long series of Spanish civil wars was not exceptional.

We may conclude that, once the great powers of Europe were organized in a concert, intervention developed into an accepted feature of international society. And also that the most effective way to impose curbs on internal freedom of action, while preserving the essence of independence, has been collective intervention by a concert of great powers.

The League, and 'the opinions of mankind' which it aimed to reflect, did weaken the legitimacy of a state's sovereign and unilateral decision to resort to force as the ultimate argument in disputes with other states. But in practice the restraints imposed by the League's version of collective security turned out to be quite inadequate. Two principal deficiencies warn us of what to avoid in future. The strongest powers were not committed to the League; and the concept of 'aggression' involved a commitment to defend the territorial status quo imposed by the victors,[3] without meaningful machinery either for territorial adjustment or for collective intervention in the internal affairs of member states. It is possible to see the League's European 'peace' as a long cease-fire leading to World War II.

Fortunately territory is now a less primary issue than it was. Technology makes it possible for advanced industrial economies like Japan, Germany and Britain to function successfully without territorial control of markets and sources of food and raw materials, so long as peace and order ensure their access to these necessities. In Europe sovereignty is being steadily surrendered: the French and German governments argue not about Alsace–Lorraine but about interest rates. Independent ex-colonies in Africa and elsewhere are not eager to expand their territory: they are determined to preserve the territorial boundaries they inherited from the Europeans. But the conflicts in Bosnia and Palestine are reminders of the passions that territorial disputes can still arouse, and of the case for restraint hegemonially imposed from outside.

In the interests of peace and order, and no less of human rights and the environment, we may welcome the changes in the concept of independence.

A CONCERT OF ALL GREAT POWERS

Let us now turn from the aims of our present mild hegemonial authority to its means and working methods.

Perhaps the most useful lesson we can draw from the failure of the League is that a hegemonial concert can contribute meaningfully to the management of international society only if it includes all the effective power centres, however informally. France under its revolutionary and Napoleonic governments may have behaved outrageously in the view of the other major powers; but these powers all saw that their concert needed to include a re-legitimized France, because of its manifest strength and its contributions to European civilization. The co-option of France stands in contrast to the unwisdom of the treatment of Weimar Germany after the First World War. But after the war against Hitler Western Germany was quickly incorporated as a major element in the Western system; similarly, the Soviets incorporated Eastern Germany. The United States also acted responsibly in the Pacific: it allowed and encouraged Japan to occupy a prominent position in the economic structure of the non-Communist world, while restraining it to a minor military role. The Western great powers face the same test of responsible statesmanship today with regard to the place of Russia and increasingly China in their concert.

We can therefore identify the need for all the major powers to consult with one another regularly and at the highest levels, accepting a certain balance among themselves. They need to agree on and jointly enforce collective hegemonial policies, or at least acquiesce in them. And their concert needs to be more flexible than for instance the Concert of Europe whose members all belonged to the same *grande république*. It must be elastic enough to allow for different cultural assumptions as well as disagreements on policy, since they will not all always agree. Fortunately the major powers recognize this need, at least on most issues. Since the end of the cold war the five permanent members of the Security Council and the G7/G8 between them involve all the major powers except perhaps India.

THE CASE FOR DELEGATED RESPONSIBILITY

On a more practical plane, a given operation of the concert will work more smoothly if one or more hegemonial powers take the lead, and decide its scope and limits and how to apply the restraints. More often than not it is expedient to delegate responsibility for co-ordinating pressure, and especially forceful intervention, to one major power.

Here it is useful to quote from a thoughtful attempt by the Indian scholar, Professor A.P. Rana, to make a realistic diagram of how international society and world order are evolving. Rana's pioneering essay is especially interesting because it comes from one of the great Asian centres of civilization, which is in the process of gradually assuming a position on the world stage commensurate with its size and capacities.

Rana first describes the hegemonial world consortium of donors, which he calls the New Northern Concert of Powers (a much larger group of states than what I have called the hegemonial concert). Rana sees the Northern Concert as still evolving and nebulous, but already extending from North America through Europe and Russia to Japan. Its various members are linked together by a common approach to international economic organization, and have a common interest in managing the numerous conflicts of the Third World.

> As a result of the tightening mesh of interdependence none of the units of the NNCP can act singly, nor can they divide into groups pitted one against another; and none of them [has the] ability to play the part of an international hegemon in maintaining international order. This leads them to a kind of 'unassailable' homogeneity, enabling them to function collectively as an international hegemon in the wider anarchical system.

By contrast Rana's picture of the 'Developing South' (what I in Chapter 4 called dependent states and quasi states) is as disheartening as that of the North is encouraging.[4] In blunt terms he describes the governments and societies of most of the world as quite unable to cope unaided with a long 'list of formidable ills and problems' which it is very much in the interest of the NNCP to help correct.

Having thus set the stage, Rana then spells out in constructive terms his understanding of how the Northern hegemony will tend to work, in terms of collective and delegated responsibility.

What sort of concert, then, is this likely to be, especially if there is a move towards hegemony? Perhaps some sort of teenmurti[5] or three-faced entity. We have already identified two of its faces, a kind of Transatlantic–Pacific Rim pax, and a U.N. pax. These represent the more participatory dimensions of the role of Europe and others within the NNCP. What, however, of its more recessive role [i.e., what has been described as leadership by one or more great powers and acquiescence by the others]? This is a little too inchoate for any kind of firm delineation, but is likely to be played through one form or another of delegation – a pax delegata so to speak. The delegation could take the form of support for the interests of a stabilizing political or economic power in a particular geographical region, or for a power or group of powers, or for regional associations cogent enough to regulate order\peace\ security in the region as a whole or perhaps across regions. Or the delegation could take the form of encouraging regional balances of power which promise stability in a turbulent area. It might or might not take the form of support for a regional hegemon, depending on the latter's ability to maintain regional order without moving too far from hegemony in the direction of dominion. Support could be delegated through international funding agencies like the World Bank and the IMF. . . . The face of pax delegata is still obscure, a projection into the future. It is too early after the demise of the previous international order for the guardians of the new one which is beginning to supplant it to take stock of the complexity of the modern world and fashion particular instruments to bring order to it.[6]

I do not need to add anything to this passage. It is close enough to my own thinking.

The donors, direct and indirect, are clearly a wider group than the hegemonial concert. But the contributions of the donors need orchestrating if they are to prove effective. Collective inducements and pressures are largely determined by what the hegemonial powers can agree among themselves to use. The means of inducement used by hegemonial powers are chiefly positive. Positive pressure usually takes the form of aid: of course money, but also know-how and other assistance. The positive means of inducement have the additional advantage for the donors that they help a dependent state to achieve the standards of civilization set by the donor powers and agencies. Aid also helps recipient governments to retain the consent, or even the approval, of the governed: partly because it benefits the population at large, and partly because it provides governments with a source of patronage. Negative economic pressure, which usually takes the form of sanctions, is effective only if it is generally applied. Unilateral economic sanctions do not have much effect unless a state is very dependent on one market or donor. The ultimate form of prsssure, armed intervention, is apt to be both costly and dangerous. Also the attitude of the media and public opinion, especially when there are casualties, makes the use of force politically risky for a democratic government to undertake. But in spite of these disadvantages it remains an option for members of the concert. When using force, the concert powers and those contributing small contingents alike welcome the added respectability of UN endorsement and blue berets for their troops where that legitimation is obtainable.

One advantage of delegated authority is that not all action by a concert power needs to be reduced to the level of highest common agreement. A leader in an area can act substantially alone but with the consent and authorization of its partners and other states. American military activities in the Caribbean and Central America, for instance in Haiti, Russian ones in the Caucasus and Central Asia, and French ones in Africa, are evidence of an informal pax delegata already in operation. The legitimation of such actions, and the need for the concert power to moderate its objectives in order to obtain general or majority endorsement, is one of the present restraining functions of the United Nations.

THE ROLE OF OMNILATERAL INSTITUTIONS

The hegemonial supranational authority which I suggested at the end of Chapter 6, and which others like Professor Rana also suggest, is not at all the same thing as giving more power to a reconstructed United Nations, or other wishful forms of world government. Voting in the present General Assembly, where the largest members represent over ten thousand times more people than the smallest, produces grotesquely disproportionate and unenforceable recommendations, in spite of the leverage of the donor powers over the votes of the weakest states.[7]

However Wilson's core idea was not an embryo world government, but a limited omnilateral organization. It flourishes today. The United

Nations is in essence a permanent congress of ambassadors representing the governments of almost all independent states;[8] and it also provides machinery through which the hegemonial authority of the major powers can act. It is true that the cold war made a collective concert impossible. But as explained in Chapter 3, decolonization and the tripling of its membership have given the UN new and valuable secondary functions. One important function is to legitimize and make more palatable the limits imposed by the hegemonial concert on the external and internal independence of member states. The UN is today an essential part of the structure of international society.

There are many proposals for minor changes to the United Nations. Some are very desirable, but they will not alter its basic function. The main error of popular thinking about the League and the United Nations has been to overestimate their ability to manage international society, and to blame them for not doing what they cannot reasonably be expected to do. This is the error of unrealistic expectations, which is one of the besetting problems of democracies.[9] Fortunately few people responsible for the conduct of world affairs any longer make this mistake about the United Nations. But it is still widespread in Western popular thinking and in criticisms by the media. A sieve is a useful instrument: it is not reasonable to blame it for not holding water, or to try to make it waterproof.

RESTRAINTS ON HEGEMONIAL POWERS

Some degree of hegemony is always present in societies towards the multiple independences end of the spectrum. It is therefore always appropriate to ask what limits restrain the hegemonial power or powers. In a world that is becoming increasingly inter-involved, especially economically, there will certainly be restraints on the freedom of action of even the strongest powers. First, there are the impersonal restraints imposed by the states system itself, which will become stronger as the net grows tighter and the system more interactive. These restraints are not only economic: the prospect of mutual nuclear annihilation deterred the superpowers even during the hostility of the cold war. Second, when there is a concert, as there is today, the thinking and policies of each concert power are continuously influenced and modified by the dialogue and negotiation with the other concert powers on a variety of issues, and by joint implementation of agreed action. Personal meetings between the political leaders greatly increase their influence on each other. Such meetings were rare in the days of the Concert of Europe, but modern transport makes them a regular practice. We can see this process at work in the discussions of the G7, and in the 'control groups' for particular problems like Bosnia and Iraq.[10] A third limit to the effective independence of responsible great powers is *raison de système*: they see the advantage to themselves of exercising their hegemonial authority with the minimum of coercion and constraint, in ways that are as acceptable to other states as possible. What Rana calls the Northern Concert will want to act where practicable within the legitimacies and conventions prized by the governing elites of the Developing South, especially sovereign independence.

In the present phase most of the great powers are willing to work out compromises for concerted action, occasionally disagreeing but acquiescing. They do not individually have the power, or the will, to block action by the concert; they see that flexible co-operation will give them much, though not all, of what they want. This is the case with Japan and Germany, and with Russia, France and Britain. But two of today's major powers, the United States and China, are more committed to unilateral policies and action. It is a matter of degree. Both American and Chinese policy-makers are of course aware of the advantages of compromise and co-operation; but both think of themselves less as members of a team or concert of major powers, and more as leaders of great and unique independent states. They are therefore less willing to brook limits on their independence except those that they may choose to impose on themselves. The mythology and indeed the historical reality of both countries portrays them as freeing themselves from the shackles of colonialism. Both resent attempts by outsiders, whether a concert of great powers or 'the international community', to control or modify even their external policies, and more so any attempt to interfere in their internal affairs.

The United States is much the most influential state in the world today. Its global reach is so great that some Americans and others see it as exercising a 'unipolar' hegemony. In many areas, such as the Americas and the Middle East, it prefers to exercise its hegemonial authority alone; but in general, and especially in economic management, American statesmen prefer to act as leaders of the hegemonial concert. American policies carry so much weight that they inevitably attract a large volume of governmental and public comment and criticism from all around the world. Some of the criticism expresses irritation at American arrogance, especially on moral issues is anti-hegemonial. It is heard even from fellow members of the concert. Suns of glory, said Alexander Pope, please not till they set. We saw that American efforts to change the domestic governance of other states in order to promote human rights are particularly resented by many governments. Criticism of a different kind, that the United States supports reactionary governments against their supposedly leftist peoples, still echoes from the cold war in left-wing circles, especially about Central America and Vietnam. Other criticism reflects resentment against private US corporations rather than against the government. The criticism and resentment acts as a check and balance. It helps to restrain American freedom of action, and makes the United States more willing to act in concert with other great powers. Moreover much of it is understandable, and some of it indeed justified, especially in the case of some private companies. Every known hegemony has had a negative side. In fields like human rights judgement is necessarily subjective. Only on balance and in comparison with others can we say that American hegemony is more beneficial than most.

The compromises needed for concert powers to agree or acquiesce among themselves are often considerable. The costs of sustained hegemonial management all round the world (whether by means of carrots or sticks), are heavy. The task of conciliating and persuading the majority of states is endless and usually only partly successful. These three restraints impose very real limits on the freedom of action of any concert of the largest powers in a system.

TODAY AND TOMORROW

The framework of relations between states in Chapter 1 left us with two sets of questions. The first set concerned the role of hegemony in the present phase of relations between states. The second concerned current assumptions about independence and the prospects for greater supranational authority. In a broad sense, both are aspects of the central question of this book: what are the present limits of independence, and are these limits likely to increase?

In today's world hegemony is one of the major limitations on the freedom of action of nominally independent states. We saw that a degree of hegemony is always present in state systems near the multiple independences end of the spectrum, because in such conditions some states are much more powerful than others. Systems that move along the spectrum towards greater centralization are usually impelled by their strongest power or powers, which acquire increasing control even though the rules and institutions of the society may disguise the reality. But the strongest states do not retain freedom of action: they too become entangled in the management process.

Other governments in the main accept hegemonial authority, though sometimes reluctantly. Anti-hegemonial rhetoric and the glorification of independence are often an alibi or cover-story complying with hegemonial demands. The governments of most states, and public opinion in the Western donor countries, recognize the effectiveness of the inducements and restraints which the hegemonial powers can and do bring to bear in order to promote peace, prosperity and human rights; they rely to a considerable extent on the aid and other inducements offered by Rana's wider NNCP. They look in particular to the United States, the only power with a global reach. Moreover there is a general awareness among governments that without hegemonial authority the world as we know it would be a dangerous place. To rely merely on the restraints engendered by involvement in the system and by the formal laws and institutions of the society has proved disastrously insufficient in the twentieth century. And no other adequate curbs on freedom of action are available.

The Western great powers take their hegemonial responsibility seriously enough by and large. But they tend to regard the responsibility as theirs to determine. They have not yet worked out how to co-opt the great Asian powers, whose weight in the scales is rapidly growing. Japan alone of the great Asian states has made much progress in learning to co-operate in a collective hegemony. And we have seen that an effective collective hegemony needs to bring in all the great powers, even if they do not always agree with the compromises and give-and-take which joint action requires. Moreover many people in the smaller as well as the larger states look to the hegemonial West for more active promotion of peace, prosperity and rights. Such people fear, understandably, that a comprehensive collective authority which included China would disagree more and achieve less than a more limited group of powers sharing the same goals and led by the United States. One possible consolation may be that our general inability to see the future, or even the consequences of our own actions, is such that when in doubt it is probably better to do too little than too much.

In this atmosphere of a hegemony that observes the forms of independence, most of the smaller states – the recipient half of the recipient–donor list – are particularly concerned with economic advantages, especially money. They, as well as the individual donor states and the international donor agencies, are steadily becoming more sophisticated about the techniques of aid as a permanent institution, and the conditions of giving and taking it. As a result the donor–recipient relationship is becoming symbiotic, built into the economies of both sides. The institutionalization of aid has clearly moved international practice some way from multiple independences. But it has not so far shifted the legitimacy of independence. On the contrary, *de jure* or legal sovereignty and the symbols and trappings of independence seem likely to remain a key element in making aid, and the economic and non-economic conditions of aid, acceptable to states that have newly emerged from colonial subordination but are still dependent in practice. The co-option of Asian great powers into a collective hegemony would reinforce the importance of respect for nominal independence. In other words, it would shift the legitimacy of the international society a little way back towards anarchy, but probably leave the practice much as it is now.

And what of tomorrow? We have seen that, in answer to the second set of questions, the conventional assumptions about independence and sovereignty in 'inter-national' relations are out of date, and that the present limits to independence are already greater than those assumptions provide for. Are the restraints becoming tighter still? And will we be better off in mundane advantages if they are?

An underlying theme of this book has been that the practice of our society of states has recently moved some way along the spectrum from the theoretical absolute of anarchical independences; that about half the states in the world are in varying degrees of dependence; and that our fairly hierarchical society of states is managed, not ideally but adequately, by an informal collective hegemony of the greatest powers. The pendulum is now moving through that area of hegemony that lies between what can properly be called an international structure and a supranational one.

Given that our practice is changing, to what extent are our ideas of what is legitimate, and desirable, changing with it? About that I am less sure. Perhaps they are changing more than we realize. We are coming to think more in terms of a collective, and therefore central and supranational, responsibility for the mundane benefits that are beyond the capacity of nation–states to achieve alone. Peace and the environment both obviously belong in this category. We have come in the last fifty years to accept that prosperity too transcends the individual state.

So far as peace is concerned, we may agree that the restraints on freedom of action, even of the greatest powers, are stronger than the legitimacy and the conventional wisdom say. Some of the restraints on great powers operate through fear of the consequences of imprudent behaviour, while others are moral and voluntary. They are sufficient in the present phase. But those who remember the first half of the century, and others too, must wonder how much reliance can be placed on them when circumstances change. The same need for stronger collective action also applies to prosperity and to the protection of the environment. The impersonal pressures of economics and weaponry and information, largely driven by human inventiveness and private enterprise – in other words by technological advance – and not by the governments of states, are inexorably tightening the net that binds us, so that it becomes harder for any state to escape from its toils.

As the net tightens, peace, prosperity, human rights and the environment stand out as the issues at stake, especially for the West; and most non-Western countries would add independence and the maintenance of internal order. The translation of these aims into practice is controversial. I have set out in this book the case for moving along the spectrum out of an international system tempered by hegemony and into a system with an adequate supranational authority. That case seems to me as compelling for the world as it is or was for Europe, and perhaps more so. Such a supranational authority does not exist today. Nor, short of a major catastrophe, will it suddenly be called into being. How then is such a change likely to come about, if it does?

Many experts on the subject and the majority of concerned Western opinion hope that stronger collective control can be achieved by individual states voluntarily surrendering more of their powers to multilateral and where possible omnilateral federal authorities. Voluntary centralization can certainly be achieved by groups of states with the same culture, the same political background and the same stage of development, such as the thirteen British colonies in North America or the European *grande république*. But effective supranational authority over the whole of our vastly diverse global system seems to me very unlikely to be achieved by non-hegemonial means. For a period of years at least, movement along the spectrum is likely to result from closer **informal co-operation and involvement of the major powers**. The collective hegemony may gradually establish itself as a supranational authority, more effective on some issues than others. What is at present an informal concert will perhaps gradually become institutionalized and codified,[11] with a legitimacy that accords due respect to nominal independence and provides for assent by other ever less independent states. If the pendulum keeps swinging in its present direction, the great powers, and especially the US, are likely to become increasingly **the joint trustees and executors of a general will of mankind.**

NOTES

1 Even in this area of the spectrum, crusades or jihads and other attempts to spread a set of values occur.

2 Technology is not just machines, but the social organization and attitudes that go along with them. New technology develops only within a suitable matrix, and as it develops it transforms social organizations, in Western as well as Eastern countries. The Japanese have adapted themselves to new technology produced in the West as quickly and as well as the Americans, and certainly as the British or the Russians, and are now making their own major contribution. Similarly in the Indian sub-continent, from the introduction of gunnery into India by Muslims and European traders down to the sophisticated technology of today, the relevant segments of Hindu society have shown a remarkable adaptability to new techniques. However, there is a significant academic debate about the transfer of technology from one culture to another.

3 The ancient Greeks had a pertinent story about the dangers of commitment to the status quo and blindness to the need and inevitability of change. The citizens of Locris, it was said, thought their laws so good and just that they declared that the laws could never be changed, and those who did not like them could leave. And now, it was said, there is no one living in Locris.

4 In a striking passage, Rana says:

> Substantial areas of the NNCP have emerged from the thraldom of nationalism and conventional national sovereignties. . . . In the Developing South however, nationalisms are fervid and divisive, and increasingly incongruent with state boundaries. State building and regime legitimation are major tasks still to be accomplished amid continual upheavals, with the phenomenon of the 'ethnie' (that complex compound of cultural, social and associated assertions) preempting the possibility of stable formations. Endemic intra-state conflict on a wide variety of fronts, with associated regional links and support, often spills over into international conflict, and coercion is more often than not employed to deal with it. Coercive politics abounds. Problems of economic development, of social class, of language, religion, shared historical experience, of race and kinship, of state boundaries arbitrarily imposed by departing colonial powers, of the necessity to satisfy human needs and human rights and build a civil society, are endemic in most developing areas. These are compounded by issues of population and ecology, the ravages of terrorism, an adverse civil–military nexus, the diversion of resources to arms production and the cost of arms transfers, dissatisfied expectations of good governance and of economic well-being consequent on the transnationalizing influence of global communications, not to mention the cultural traumas that the latter cause by throwing variegated and diverse peoples with ancient memories and traditions too close together too quickly for their own comfort – here is a list of formidable ills and problems which, if unattended by any scheme to bring about order, could prove to be prohibitively costly for the world as a whole.

So bleak a description of the dependent states is likely to come only from candid Asians. A Westerner using such language would be condemned as racist and arrogant. But even Rana says 'Perhaps this is too stark a picture.'

5 Teenmurti is a Hindu diety with three aspects. I think Rana has in mind, among others, the monumental three-faced Shiva on Elephanta Island off Bombay.

6 See A.P. Rana, 'The New Northern Concert of Powers in a World of Multiple Independences', in *Regime Transformations and Global Realignments*, K. Ajuha, H. Coppens and H. van der Wusten (eds), Sage, 1993.

7 To make voting reflect population, regardless of other factors, would create equal difficulties. The donor powers, and particularly the United States, would be outvoted by large majorities but the donors include the strongest and least coercible powers. Even if China and India are co-opted into the hegemonial concert, there would still be strengthened demand for redistributing to the poorer states a much greater proportion of the wealth generated by the richer ones than the donors are now likely to give, or would be in the foreseeable future. It seems to me fortunate that present efforts to establish supranational authority are mainly hegemonial, with the United Nations as a legitimating and moderating factor.

8 Switzerland and Taiwan are conspicuous non-members. A few member states do not have effective governments for their ambassadors to represent: at the time of writing, Afghanistan, Somalia and Liberia are examples. These exceptions do not alter the general picture.

9 People running for public office often declare aims and make promises that are virtually impossible to implement, for fear that if they do not, they will lose out to others who do. The media in their role as critics emphasize what has not been achieved rather than what has, and induce the public to believe that much more could be achieved internationally than is in fact the case. Those in authority need to educate the public not to expect more than is practicable. But that is a thankless task.

10 One difficulty here for democratic countries [that we noted in Chapter 6] is that the will of the majority of the electorate, influenced by the media, is not likely to move in the same directions, or as fast, as the governments are pulled by dialogue and negotiation with other powers. Democratic governments will tend to adapt their actions and policies to fit the compromises worked out between the great powers, but will trim their rhetoric to the winds of their domestic public opinion. As a result the difference between their rhetoric and their actions will seem undemocratic. Kimon the Athenian leader in the time of the diarchy with Sparta told his demos that it was yoked to the Spartans in the management of Hellas, and an ox must not kick against its yokefellow. But the Athenian demos lost patience with its diarchy partner, with tragic results.

11 The practice of a concert needs to remain elastic and able to adapt to new problems; it is therefore desirable not to codify the practice into inflexible laws, but to leave it rather as a recognized but provisional and evolving code of conduct. Codification has the advantages of regularizing and legitimizing practice, and legitimacy is the lubricating oil of government. As collective authority increases from its present rather low level, it will be harder for it to remain flexible.

Glossary

Ahistoricism is not merely ignorance of history: in our context, the history of relations between political entities. It also means the opinion that the past is irrelevant, or almost irrelevant, to the study of international relations today, and should be disregarded in favour of, for example, algebraic calculation. In my opinion ahistoricism in the study of international relations is rather like a doctor trying to diagnose a patient without asking about the past history of his symptoms, whether other members of the family suffer from them, etc.

Anarchy in the theoretical and technical sense does not mean disorder as such. It means a situation where political units do not acknowledge any higher authority. Anarchy is often used in a sense akin to sovereignty and independence, and allows for the pressures caused by involvement in a system of states and the rules consciously put in place by an international society. Hence the title of Hedley Bull's classic work of political theory, *The Anarchical Society,* and Gilpin's 'global anarchy'. But total anarchy is a theoretical absolute: once states are involved with each other, it does not exist in practice.

Anarchophilia/-phobia Anarchophilia is the belief that states and would-be states ought to be independent, with no overarching supranational authority over them. In Buzan's words, it is the disposition to assume that the structure of the international system has always been anarchic, that this is natural, and (more selectively) that this is a good thing. Anarchophobia means the opposite: a fear of the dangers of multiple independences, and a desire for a strong overarching authority. Anarchophobia is a major impulse towards a federal Europe.

Authority here means the ability of an individual or government (or in other contexts a constitition or a church) to enlist voluntary obedience, without the use of coercion or force. It is akin to legitimacy; but a legitimate government may command little authority, and actual authority may not be legitimate. Insofar as a government depends on force to ensure compliance, it lacks authority. This political use of the word *auctoritas* seems to have been invented by Augustus to describe his ability to get his fellow senators and others to follow his lead freely without coercion. However, one strain of modern liberal thought persists in maintaining a dichotomy between authority and freedom.

Balance of Power was originally a bankers' metaphor. In a system of substantially independent states it rejects supranational authority; but it goes beyond mere anti-hegemonial coalitions against the strongest power, and aims to preserve independence and hold all strong powers in check by maintaining an equilibrium. A balance requires constant adjustment as states grow stronger or weaker, and requires the states concerned to have no permanent allies or enemies. Maxims such as that the enemy of today will be the ally of tomorrow derive from the balance of power. A just balance of power in for instance the Utrecht settlement of 1714 does not mean conformity with an abstract notion of justice such as self-determination or hereditary legitimacy, but rather a balance that must be kept adjusted.

Capitulations were originally the codifications (arrangement in capitula or chapters) of agreements between the Ottoman empire and European states regulating matters such as trade. At first largely determined by the Ottomans, they gradually became biased in favour of the Europeans as these grew stronger, and became the basis for similiar arrangements in countries like China. States involved in a system need arrangements to regulate trade, warfare, diplomacy and so on; examples of such arrangements are found as early as those between the Egyptian pharaohs and the Hittite kings. Such cross-cultural regulations are usually value-free and much looser than the rules, institutions and codes of conduct that govern an international society.

Coercion and Voluntary Agreement Coercion in international relations is sometimes used to describe only military compulsion, the use of force. Coercion is also widely used, as in this book, to include other kinds of pressure or negative persuasion, such as economic sanctions, denial of aid and breaking of diplomatic relations. The inducements used by rich and powerful states to get other states to conform to their wishes – the carrots and sticks of hegemonial diplomacy – are normally a mixture of coercion in the wider sense and voluntary agreement. Even in the most positive diplomatic language there is a tacit note of 'or else'. At present the use of force except with UN authorization is generally condemned. There is increasing emphasis on moving the global international society, or groups of states in it, along the spectrum away from multiple independences by means of voluntary associations and unions.

A hegemony, whether unitary or collective, normally has some elements of both coercion and voluntary agreement. So do the rules and institutions of an international society. Those of the European society were far from purely voluntary: they were to a considerable extent imposed by the victors at the great peace settlements. Today small, weak and new states want to join the international society because membership legitimizes their nominal independence, and they accept the limitations imposed by the hegemony of the great powers.

Concert of Powers means a diffused or collective hegemony of a number of major powers when no member is strong enough to overule the others. A concert requires the great powers that form it to agree or acquiesce on actions jointly carried out and actions delegated to one or more powers. Because it is collective it incorporates elements of a balance of power, and its decisions are usually more acceptable to other states than those of a single hegemonial power. To be effective a concert needs to include all the major powers in a society such as Europe, not just the victors in the last major war. Whether a concert or collective hegemony composed of all the major powers can operate in the present worldwide multicultural society is an open question.

Dominion covers that part of the spectrum between suzerainty and centralization where a central or imperial authority to some extent determines the internal government of other political entities, but they nevertheless retain their identity and some control over their own affairs. But in practice some ability to determine a dependent state's internal affairs, such as today's hegemonial concert is able to exercise, is not dominion.

Empire and imperial are traditional and convenient names for the centralized end of the spectrum. Historically most moves away from multiple independences towards central or supranational authority have been imperial in the conventional sense, but they can be substantially voluntary, by means of leagues and unions. Therefore some scholars call the theoretical ends of the spectrum anarchy and hierarchy.

Eurocentric means a view of the world which focuses on Europe and takes European ideas for granted: in our context particularly over human rights, social values, and the relations of Europeans with the rest of mankind. Eurocentrism is partly a cultural limitation of perspective. The view that only the European experience is relevant to international relations today is a form of ahistoricism. Eurocentrism is at present much out of favour in the English-speaking world, and also but less so in continental Europe.

Grande République refers to the states that grew out of Latin Christendom; and by extension all Christian European states. Voltaire described Europe as one great republic, give or take Russia, divided into several states (or estates); Gibbon said that a philosopher (or presumably a student of international relations) may be permitted to consider Europe as one great republic. Europe was a cultural unity, and its international society was formed within the matrix of that culture. Heeren, writing in Napoleon's time, defined what he called a states system and we call an international society as a union of several contiguous states resembling each other in their manners, religion and degree of social improvement, and cemented together by a reciprocity of interests. While Europe was and is a grande république, our global society of states is far from meeting Heeren's criteria.

Hegemony in a society of largely independent states means the ability of the most powerful states to determine the nature of the society, and especially its practice. In theory a single hegemonial power or concert of powers can determine (to a varying extent) the external behaviour of other states in the society, but not their internal conduct. In practice the line between influencing external and internal conduct has always been smudged, and today is particularly so. Some degree of hegemonial practice is an integral factor of societies near the anarchic end of the spectrum. What makes other states accept or at least tolerate hegemonial authority is not only their inability to change it. Hegemonial practice, especially when it is collective and based on balanced compromises, provides greater elasticity than international law or majority voting, and injects a valuable dose of international order into what would otherwise be a free-for-all. Consequently the degree of central or hegemonial authority is often considerably greater in practice than the theoretical legitimacy provides for. This is the case today.

Hierarchy is a term sometimes used as the opposite of anarchy to describe the centralized or imperial end of the spectrum. The term avoids the coercive overtones of empire; but a hierarchy implies a gradation of states or authorities as in a priesthood or business corporation, whereas a centralized state may be unitary rather than strictly hierarchical in the sense of one political entity ruling another.

Human Rights grew out of the concept of the rights of man. The term now usually refers to the United Nations universal declaration on human rights (see Chapter 5). That declaration, and most of the activity of private human rights organizations, is based on Western concepts of these rights. These human rights are designed to protect the individual citizen against the state or local authority, but not against omnilateral bodies like the UN. They fall into two categories: interferences from which governments ought to refrain, and benefits which governments ought to provide (see Chapter 5 for details). Most governments of newly constituted and fragile states, and much marxist thought, stress the rights of communities rather than individuals.

Independence Independent states today are no longer only those that can stand on their own feet without being dependent on others. Independence no longer means absolute control of foreign and domestic policy. Rather it is a status or legitimacy which has been conferred on a large number of states, mostly former dependencies, and which – like sovereignty – leaves every such state a degree of local autonomy. The nature of nominal independence in states that are in practice dependent is discussed in Chapter 4.

International Society The political entities involved in a system of states bring some order into their dealings with one another by gradually working out rules and institutions to manage their relations. In some cases the machinery is purely regulatory (see **Capitulations**). Where the rules and institutions are sufficiently coherent, and backed up by some shared values such as a common religion, and by a code of conduct that the members normally observe, we can speak of an international society in the looser half of the spectrum, and a supranational one in the tighter half. All international societies that we know of have been formed within the matrix of a single culture. But as Butterfield observed, once an international society in this sense 'is already in existence, it may not be difficult to add to it new units which were once outside it – even units that are of a quite alien culture'. A society, we say, legitimizes the behaviour and the relations between its members that it approves. In different societies at different times the legitimacy is found over a wide range of the spectrum.

Legitimacy in general means being in accordance with law or principle. In the European society of princes it derived from a prince being the rightful heir of his or her predecessor. Today it refers to a state being recognized as juridically independent and equal with other states in international law. The legitimacy of a system or society of states means the degree of independence and supranational authority (the position in the spectrum), and the rules and institutions, which the members publicly recognize as valid and binding. In most systems the legitimacy differs from the practice. In our case it differs considerably.

Nation is a confusing word. Derived from the Latin to be born, its basic meaning is a distinct race or people, marked off by common descent, or language, or history, or living together in a state such as the United States. In this sense the Italians for instance were a nation before there was an Italian state, and Prussia was described as always a state and never a nation. Unfortunately nation is also used, especially in North America, to mean an independent state, as in United Nations, and also in words such as nationality meaning citizenship of a state, and international meaning inter-state.

Political Entity is a wider term than state, especially in contexts where states, and in American usage nations, are assumed to be independent. An example is the Palestinian Arabs, who at present are obviously a political entity but not a state. The term can also be applied to constituted provinces, especially those that see themselves as separate such as perhaps Quebec. It is better to avoid using the term to include political parties, etc. that have no governmental functions as such.

Raison d'Etat in Europe from the seventeenth century meant the calculation of a state's interests, a right and reason that recognized a ruler's obligations to all those committed to his or her charge. It held that the interests of the state take precedence over obligations to other states and sometimes moral obligations. *Raison de système*, the view that the rules and institutions of an international society promote the interests of a state (or of all states), developed out of *raison d'état*.

Raison de Système In a non-hegemonial society of independent states, such as prevailed in Europe in the eighteenth century, *raison de système* involves respecting the rules of the society and above all maintaining what the Utrecht settlement called a just balance of power. Where there is a collective hegemony, as in nineteenth-century

Europe, *raison de système* requires the hegemonial powers to observe an adequately co-operative balance between themselves and to ensure that other states too make the system work. Where the hegemony is exercised by a single power, *raison de système* involves exercising it in a way that brings advantages to the hegemonial power itself and to all or most other powers in the system: for otherwise an anti-hegemonial coalition will form. There is no unseen hand or guarantee that *raison de système* will prevail in any of these circumstances. On the contrary it requires statesmanship of a high order among many powers, and especially restraint by hegemonial powers. The record of the European society of states from about 1650 (Westphalia) to about 1900 (the slide towards World War I) is remarkable for the long periods, except for Napoleon, during which *raison de système* prevailed, though the necessary adjustments to change sometimes involved minor wars. In those periods the strongest powers were not only limited by the pressures of the system but were also responsible enough to show an adequate minimum of voluntary restraint.

Responsibility in international affairs has several meanings, which are defined at the beginning of Chapter 6.

The **Spectrum** is a notional range of ways of organizing a system of states, from absolute anarchy or multiple independences to total centralization or empire. All known systems, and the rules of their regulation or government, fall somewhere along the spectrum; the two extremes are theoretical and are not found in practice. Historically systems have moved back and forth along the spectrum over time. In diverse or conglomerate imperial structures like those of Napoleon or Augustus, and hegemonial arrangements like the recipient–donor list described in Chapter 7, various political entities occupy different positions along the spectrum at the same time, from unitary centralization to independence. For a comparison of the spectrum for a states system with that for the internal government of a state see Chapter 7.

State (like nation) is a confusing word. In the USA a state means by historical accident a province of the federal state, which is therefore usually called a nation. For over a century Canada has been described as two nations in the bosom of a single state. In British imperial language some Asian and other autonomous entities were called native states. Since a state in the sense of a constituted government is a fundamental concept of current political theory generally and of international (i.e., inter-state) relations in particular, it is an indispensable word. It should be used with precision, and not interchangeably with nation.

States are not necessarily independent, even nominally. There are various categories of dependent state (for instance colonies, U.N. trusteeships) and degrees of dependence, in theory and in practice. Dependent states contribute to the pressures of the states system as a whole. Yet much international theory and some international law concerns itself only with nominally independent states.

Suzerainty in general means that one state exercises some political control over another; sometimes a shadowy overlordship that amounts to little in practice. Some theorists of international relations call suzerain systems and societies those in which the members accept hegemony as legitimate, and therefore do not claim sovereign independence. At Waever's suggestion I have used it in this book to mean the midpoint in the spectrum between multiple independences and total centralization.

System of States When a number of political entities are closely and inextricably involved with one another, we call the group a states system (as we speak of a solar system). The differing patterns of relationship between the states in a system range along a spectrum between two theoretical extremes: absolute independence of all the political entities involved, and the equally theoretical extreme of absolute, unitary centralization. It is convenient to give the latter theoretical extreme its traditional name of a universal empire. But the term has pejorative overtones and centralization can be voluntary; some scholars call the theoretical ends of the spectrum anarchy and hierarchy. All known systems, that is all the patterns of which we have any record, including the present global system and the European one from which it is substantially derived, lie somewhere along the spectrum. They contain elements both of independence, which gradually becomes more limited and diluted into local autonomy as one moves along the spectrum towards centralization or empire, and of imperial control which similarly becomes diluted into looser hegemonial authority when we move the other way.

Further reading on international society

Students of international relations and other interested readers may wish to compare what I have to say on this subject, particularly in Chapter 1 and the glossary, with the following readings. I have selected them from the flood of recent writing on international and supranational societies, with the help of suggestions provided me by Professor Buzan, himself a major contributor. Some other relevant works are also cited in the notes. I have listed these readings chronologically, to illustrate the course and the liveliness of the current debate about the nature of international and supranational society.

Herbert Butterfield and Martin Wight, eds, *Diplomatic Investigations*, Allen & Unwin, 1966.

John Vincent, *Non-intervention and International Order*, Princeton University Press, 1974.

Hedley Bull, *Martin Wight and the Theory of International Relations*, British Journal of International Studies 2, 1976.

Hedley Bull, *The Anarchical Society*, Macmillan, 1977.

Martin Wight, *Systems of States*, Leicester University Press, 1977.

Kenneth Waltz, *Theory of International Politics*, Addison-Wesley, 1979.

Kenneth Thompson, on Butterfield and Wight in *Masters of International Thought*, Louisiana University Press, 1980.

Robert Gilpin, *War and Change in World Politics*, Cambridge University Press, 1981.

Hedley Bull and Adam Watson, eds, *The Expansion of International Society*, Oxford University Press, 1984.

Hedley Bull, ed., *Intervention in World Politics*, Oxford University Press 1984, (especially 'Intervention and International Law', by Dame Rosalyn Higgins).

Robert Keohane, *After Hegemony*, Princeton University Press, 1984.

Robert Keohane, ed., *Neorealism and its Critics*, Columbia University Press, 1986 (answers to Waltz).

Michael Doyle, *Empires*, Cornell University Press, 1986.

Adam Watson, *Hedley Bull, State Systems and International Societies*, Review of International Studies, 13:2, 1987.

N. Onuf and F. Klink, *Anarchy, Authority and Rule*, International Studies Quarterly 33:2, 1989.

Adam Watson, *Systems of States*, Review of International Studies, 16:2, 1990.

James Mayall, *Nationalism and International Society*, Cambridge University Press, 1990.

Gabriela Wight and B. Porter, eds, *Martin Wight – International Theory: the three traditions*, Leicester University Press, 1991.

Evan Luard, ed., *The Evolution of Ideas about International Society*, Macmillan, 1991.

Helen Milner, *The Asssumption of Anarchy in International Relations Theory*, Review of International Studies 17:1, 1991.

Alexander Wendt, *Anarchy is what States make of it*, in International Organization, 46\2, 1992.

Adam Watson, *The Evolution of International Society*, Routledge, 1992.

Barry Buzan, *From International System to International Society* in International Organization, 47\3, 1993.

J.G. Ruggie, *Territoriality and Beyond*, in International Relations 471, 1993.

Samuel Barkin and Bruce Cronin, *The State and the Nation: changing norms and the rule of sovereignty*, in International Organization 48\1, 1994.

Benjamin Miller, *Explaining the Emergence of Great Power Concerts*, Review of International Studies 204, 1994.

Richard Stubbs and Geoffrey Underhill, eds, *Political Economy and the Changing Global Order*, 1994.

Barry Buzan and Richard Little, *The Idea of 'International System'*, International Political Science Review 15\3, 1994.

James Der Derian, ed., *International Theory: critical investigations*, Macmillan, 1995 (especially foreword by Watson).

Fawn, Larkin and Newman, eds, *International Society after the Cold War*, Macmillan, 1996.

Barry Buzan and Richard Little, *Reconceptualizing Anarchy*, in the European Journal of International Relations, Volume 2\4, 1996.

Index

Adenauer, Konrad 33, 35, 36, 41
adequacy of dependence 70–5
administration 35, 39, 48–9, 51–2,
    54–5, 57–8, 60–3, 66, 71, 76–7,
    82, 84–5, 107–9, 111–12, 122,
    210–1
Africa 46, 48, 51–3, 55, 58–60, 62–4,
    66, 77, 79–80, 84, 91–2, 113, 131,
    135
agreements 7, 17, 110–11, 113–14,
    129
aid 3, 56, 61, 64, 67, 73, 75–6, 78,
    80–1, 89, 93, 102, 108–9, 113,
    115–17, 122, 128, 134–5, 139–40
alliances 98–9, 107
anarchophilia 32–9, 56, 121, 124
anarchy 3, 8–9, 16–17, 19, 26, 28–9,
    31, 40, 66–7, 85, 95, 117–18,
    121–3, 126, 128–9, 140
Angola 58, 76
anti-colonialism 83–4
aristocracy 18–19, 73
armed rebellion 57–8, 62, 107
Asia 9–11, 42, 46–9, 51–3, 55–8,
    60–3, 65–7, 84–6, 93–4, 102, 108,
    117, 129, 135, 139–40
assistance 63, 75, 115, 130, 134
Australasia 46, 65
Australia 55, 57, 107
Austria 21, 24
authority 17, 23, 84–6, 88, 115
autocracy 22, 27, 85
autonomy 1, 7, 24, 34, 61–2, 72,
    75–6, 93, 101, 104, 107, 112, 114,
    117, 119–22

balance of power 5, 10, 21, 26–7,
    40–2
Berlin Congress (1884–85) 55–6, 87
Bismarck, Otto Eduard Leopold,
    Prince von 19, 26
Bosnia 75, 92, 127, 132, 137
Britain: anti-hegemony 36; authority
    85; colonialism 10–11, 27, 48–9,
    51, 54–5, 57, 63, 65, 80, 84, 110,
    141; decolonization 57, 59–60;
    effect of World War I 29; Europe
    and 33; functioning 131; global
    relations 42; industrial revolution
    25; intervention 131; nation-state
    35–6; postwar Germany 32; power
    26–7, 137; rise of 41; slavery 87,
    129
British West Indies 60
Burke, MP for Bristol 55, 57
Buzan, Barry 3, 17

Canada 55, 57, 107
capitalism 112, 114
capitulation 99, 111, 118, 127
Caribbean 52, 58, 60, 62–4, 70,
    72–3, 78, 80, 113, 135
Central America 78, 135, 138
Central Europe 28, 35–6, 40
centralization 1–3, 7, 21–2, 66, 120,
    122, 138, 141
Charles V, Holy Roman Emperor
    106–7
China 10, 12, 49, 53, 64, 85–6,
    88–91, 93, 111, 113, 129, 132,
    137, 139